THE REAL ESTATE TEAM PLAYBOOK

OTHER BOOKS BY STEVE SHULL

Real Estate Is Not Rocket Science: The Six Core Building Blocks to Succeed in Any Market

The Full Fee Agent: How to Stack the Odds in Your Favor as a Real Estate Professional

OTHER BOOKS BY JONATHAN LACK

You Can't Scale Chaos: The Veteran Real Estate Agent's Guide to Working Smarter and Selling More

Plan to Turn Your Company Around in 90 Days: How to Restore Positive Cash Flow and Profitability

STEVE SHULL · DANA GREEN · JONATHAN LACK

THE REAL ESTATE TEAM PLAYBOOK

Work Smarter. Profit More.
Get Your Life Back.

Ballast Books, LLC
www.ballastbooks.com

Paperback ISBN: 978-1-962202-14-5
Hardcover ISBN: 978-1-962202-13-8

Printed in the United States of America

Published by Ballast Books
www.ballastbooks.com

For more information, bulk orders, appearances, or speaking requests, please email: info@ballastbooks.com

This book is dedicated to team leaders across the United States who inspire us and others with their drive and passion to be the best residential real estate agents they can be while leading a team of other agents and staff to be the best they can be.

CONTENTS

Foreword

Steve Shull saved my life.

If you're thinking this is a dramatic way to start a book about real estate, let me put it another way. In the absence of Steve's coaching and sage guidance, I would likely still be on the top-producer hamster wheel—selling a few hundred homes every year and making all the ego-boosting rankings lists, but depleted and entirely miserable. Instead, today I love my life and spend my days creating impact through my dream career.

I met Steve in 2013. "You're the real deal," he said during our initial call. He was perhaps the first person in real estate who helped me believe that phrase could be true. Steve went on to introduce me to other clients and collaborators who met that same description—people like the brilliant co-authors of this book, Dana Green and Jonathan Lack. It's rare to meet a team leader as successful as Dana, who brings vision, strategy, and empathy to her business in equal measure. As for Jonathan, you won't find a more passionate and learned advocate of simple and sound business practices. They are the real deal.

Over the years, Steve and his incomparable network of collaborators helped me crack the code to create culture, strategy, systems, and structure to lead one of the most successful teams in the country—all without working weekends! With his support as a primary driver of progress, my team eventually ran like a finely tuned machine, offering clients an impeccable experience and each member of the operation a chance to shine.

Perhaps the greatest benefit of all is that Steve helped me find my voice, tune into my innate strengths, and rise to the occasion as a leader. That life-changing work opened my head and my heart to vast possibilities, so I could live my absolute best life.

This book is designed to help you get there too. In these pages, Steve, Dana, and Jonathan outline how to bring your greatness to life through your team. They weave their varied perspectives and profound knowledge into a tactical plan shared in the illuminating and empowering chapters ahead.

I am filled with excitement and appreciation that you are taking this step to stop the chaos and step into your greatness. In reading this book, you'll glean decades of professional wisdom without having to make every mistake yourself. You'll be inspired to push yourself personally and become the leader you were destined to be. And, you never know—these pages might just save your life.

With gratitude,
Courtney Smith

Introduction

Carey was a top-producing agent in one of the nation's hottest real estate markets, doing $50 million to $60 million a year in volume. By any measure, she was a success.

She had a "team," sort of—an assistant and a buyer's agent who had one foot out the door. Effectively, though, she was operating alone . . . and she was reaching the limit of what a solo agent could do.

Like many top agents, Carey had sacrificed a great deal to get where she was. She often put in more than twelve hours a day, seven days a week. The only way to grow her business, she believed, was to work even harder. But how hard and how long can one person work?

And honestly, she didn't *want* to work harder—she wanted more balance in her life. She wanted to remember what a weekend was, to have predictable hours, and to not spend her evenings talking nervous clients off the ledge. She loved working out, taking long hikes, and doing fun things with her three grown daughters. She had no desire to make her life all about work. She was definitely in the camp of wanting to work to live and *not* live to work. This was getting harder and harder.

Yet, like most agents, Carey was competitive. It was hard not to compare her production to other top performers and think, *If they can do it, so can I.* She was deeply motivated and driven to keep reaching for more and better.

To reconcile those two conflicting urges—to grow her business *and* reclaim her life—she needed help.

Times Have Changed

Carey hit the wall that all successful agents hit eventually: it's impossible to do everything yourself. There just aren't enough hours in the day to do what it takes to get the best outcomes for your clients. Ironically, it's a problem that grows worse with success.

Sure, if you do only a handful of transactions per year (the industry average is less than four), the workload is sustainable. The money is not though. That's why the attrition rate of real estate agents is so high—most new agents leave the business within five years. To make this career work, you've got to sell more homes than the industry average . . . a lot more.

But even if you're a rock star, you'll find that about fifty transactions per year is the absolute most you can handle. And if you're selling one or more homes a week, what kind of life do you have? For most agents, the answer is zero personal life plus endless professional stress. The financial side of this equation doesn't look a whole lot better. Yes, the gross income is high, but what you take home after taxes and expenses will probably not create the financial security you are hoping for.

It wasn't always this hard. Even just a decade ago, timelines were longer and expectations were lower. A solo agent working with a cadre of trusted professionals—stagers, photographers, lenders, and so on—might have sufficient time and bandwidth to do it all and wow their clients.

But the technology explosion has changed that. Agents are at the mercy of the supercomputer in their pocket, and clients demand the same instantaneous attention and service in real estate that they get in everything else.

Now, it takes a team to get all the work done.

And in fact, teams are beginning to take over the real estate industry. Team production has exploded, and more and more agents are moving toward the team concept. In the very near future, if not right now . . .

You will either be leading a real estate team or . . .

You will be on a real estate team or . . .

You will be competing against a real estate team.

Teams are going to get bigger—some are already crossing state lines. They'll get better as more agents embrace this process. And they'll become more challenging to compete against as their market share rapidly increases. It is just a matter of how fast this is going to happen.

Right now, the real estate industry as a whole—including brokerages and associations—still isn't set up to accommodate teams in the same way it serves individual agents. The companies don't know how to make space for teams. They don't know how to pay teams. They don't know how to charge teams. They don't know how to help teams prosper.

But this is going to change fast, or teams will outgrow the companies themselves. Teams are not going away. If you start working today to build a high-performing team in your market, you stand to gain what the tech industry calls the first-mover advantage.

In other words, opportunity knocks.

Today's Teams Are Not Really Teams

Right now, real estate teams are going through a lot of growing pains in trying to figure out how to structure themselves and do business as a cohesive unit. In truth, most teams are teams in name only—often vanity projects for star agents. Everyone is running around doing their own thing, usually in a highly unorganized and dysfunctional way. Team members compete with each other, come and go as they please, and have little or no synergy.

With that kind of team, you'll work harder, make *less* money, and have *more* stress than you do now. Not exactly what you were envisioning, is it?

But here's the thing: that is *not* a real team.

On a true team, synergy is the goal. Everyone is better off within the group than outside of it, and together, you can achieve things no individual can. Instead of a free-for-all, everyone is in the same boat, rowing in the same direction, the same way, toward the same destination.

That is a team. And that's what will elevate the home-buying and home-selling process in terms of both client experience and results. The truth is, a top-performing team can achieve vastly more than any individual (or loose group of individuals) can. Most teams are barely scratching the surface of this potential, letting untold value go to waste because they don't know how to work together.

The purpose of this book is to help you avoid that fate and build a team—or join one—that can dominate the market, grow your bank account, and give you your life back.

So what are all these real estate teams doing wrong? In most cases, successful agents launch teams thinking they'll quickly garner more business. But team building doesn't work that way, and high hopes soon turn to disappointment, topped with even more stress.

Building a high-performing team demands specialized knowledge and skills that don't come naturally to many in real estate. This is an independent contractor industry—most agents have no training or experience in building and leading teams. The history books are full of star athletes who failed as coaches because the traits that helped them succeed on the field or court didn't prepare them to lead others. The same goes for real estate.

As a result, most so-called teams don't function as teams at all. They evolve organically with no framework, and that's a big problem. Where there should be synergies, well-defined roles, and accountability, there is instead constant friction. Production may go up, but no one has a life, and it could all fall apart at any moment. The leader keeps trying to do everything, so they can never take a break, let alone sell the business and retire comfortably. Nope—their last deal is their last paycheck.

On the flip side, successful teams are powerhouses that elevate everyone who touches them—especially their leaders. There has just never been a road map to show solo agents how to build teams right.

Until now.

Three Heads Are Better

When Carey hit her limits, she sought help from Steve Shull, who has been coaching top agents nationwide for over three decades. Steve is known for his game-changing approach to performance, discipline, and teamwork, and it's no wonder—as a linebacker in the NFL, he played for the Miami Dolphins under legendary coach Don Shula, earning a Super Bowl appearance along the way.

During coaching, Carey introduced Steve to Jonathan Lack, a business consultant who specializes in turning around struggling companies. In fact, he had written a book on the subject, driven by the painful experience of watching his family's multigenerational business disintegrate in his youth. When Jonathan gave Steve a copy of his book, Steve devoured it and immediately saw that nearly everything in the book was applicable to real estate. It underscored his belief that almost every agent with a team was running a failing business that needed to be turned around.

That belief was confirmed when Steve and Jonathan began working together to consult with real estate teams. As businesses, the teams were always a mess. Even on top-producing teams that looked successful at a glance, deeper investigation showed otherwise. In most cases, the most basic fundamentals of teamwork and sound business were being neglected.

That's where Dana Green came in. Like Carey, she was a coaching client of Steve's, and as Steve is quick to admit, Dana is one of the few real estate team leaders with a healthy business. She runs the top team in her market and has been in the team game for decades; when Dana created her first team, few people in real estate had even heard of the concept. No one knows the nuts and bolts of real estate teams better.

With Steve's insider view on agents' lives, Jonathan's business acumen, and Dana's team expertise, they had all the pieces of the puzzle in place to write this book: the team blueprint that real estate agents desperately need. Teams are the future of real estate, and it's time to start making them work for you.

What You'll Learn

The book is a step-by-step guide to doing real estate teams right. Once you begin your efforts to build a team, you'll encounter a thousand factors that you never had to consider when you were a solo act. There's a broad spectrum of decisions and choices you'll face. It's a very different thought process that your career as a single agent hasn't prepared you for.

We'll lay out the journey in black and white, step by step.

Part I: The Fundamentals. First, you'll learn why to create a team (and why not), and what a team really is (and isn't).

The rest of the book reflects the phases of the team development cycle, which are a lot like the phases of a professional sports team cycle.

Part II: Pre-Season Planning. This is when you make big, fundamental decisions to put your house in order before things get hectic. That includes shifting from a solo agent to a team-leader mindset, developing your team culture and brand, deciding your team structure, and defining your business strategy.

Part III: Regular Season Execution. These are the key elements that make it possible to handle high volumes of business and still deliver an outstanding client experience. They include your systems, your people, your marketing, and your ability to continuously improve.

Part IV: Post-Season Assessment. When the regular season dies down, it's time to take stock and see how well your business and your team performed.

And then the cycle begins again. Building your team isn't a simple, linear process; it's a continuous loop. Each cycle is a new opportunity to revisit past decisions and make improvements, which you'll certainly need to do as your team scales. So don't worry about getting it perfect the first time around.

Maybe you're already a team leader, and you're frustrated because your volume and profit have failed to grow as expected. Maybe you're a member of a team, and you feel like you're spinning your wheels because your talents aren't recognized or leveraged. Or perhaps you're a successful single agent who sees the writing on the wall, and you're thinking about starting a team to maximize opportunity.

Whatever your situation, this book will show you how to succeed in real estate through collaboration with others. Right now, you don't know what you don't know, and that's the most dangerous place to be. Our goal is to introduce you to the big ideas you need to be aware of.

That said, we can't provide *all* the answers. In truth, each chapter in this book could be a whole book by itself—there's far more to learn about each of these topics than we can possibly cover in these pages. Plus, there are just too many variables that depend on your situation—your role, background, market, context, and goals.

Instead of giving you answers, we'll arm you with the right questions and a framework to follow. We'll open your eyes to all the things you need to pay attention to, and you'll find out which areas are strengths or weaknesses for you. That will enable you to choose the right additional resources to guide your growth. (We'll even point you toward some of those resources on our website, performancecoachingbooks.com.)

Fair warning: this book is not for the lazy or the faint of heart. In your career to date, especially if you're a successful single agent, you've built up a set of assumptions about every aspect of the business—buyers, sellers, brokers, support staff, marketing, client satisfaction, your fellow agents, and more. We will challenge most of these assumptions. Becoming a great team leader or member will require fundamental changes, not only in your behavior but also in your beliefs. If you let yourself get stuck in the past, you'll be left in the dust.

On a high-functioning real estate team, the whole is greater than the sum of its parts. Two plus two equals five, or even ten. The sky's the limit. As Steve remembers well from his NFL days, everybody's contribution counts, whether they are marquee, on-field talent or behind the scenes.

Real estate is a tough business. In any given market, the top 1–2 percent of agents account for a huge proportion of the transactions, often 25 percent or more. To find success, you need to stay on top of how the industry is changing. If you don't form or join a thriving team, your path to success is extremely difficult.

Dana explained this recently to a rookie agent who came to an open house just in hopes of meeting her. He was lucky—as team leader, she doesn't usually do open houses (one of the perks of having a high-functioning team), but this time she was filling in for a sick team member. So this guy got to meet *the* Dana Green, the one whose name is all over town. He said getting started on his own had been rocky, and he was looking for advice.

What did she tell him? Join a great team. You learn so much faster because you have mentorship and support, and most importantly, you get to do more reps in less time. Maybe that team is where you want to stay long term, but if you have bigger ambitions, the experience of being on a team gives you an inside look at how to build and run your own team in the future.

If Carey had been fortunate enough to get that advice earlier, she might not have had to teeter on the edge of burnout before finding the right path. Working with both Steve and Jonathan, Carey set about transforming her business. That meant completely rethinking how she operated and building a strong foundation to bring on more people and create a bona fide, high-performing team.

Three years later, as this book is being written, Carey has more than doubled her sales and is working on her next double, with sales the last two years north of $150 million each year. She is working smarter and doing it with more ease and joy. It might sound too good to be true, but it was possible because she put the right people in the right places to get her life back and to be able to focus on what she does best: nurturing past client relationships and developing new ones.

This did not happen by accident. It's a direct result of applying everything you are about to learn in this book. What has worked for Carey can and will work for you if you follow the blueprint laid out for you in the following pages.

PART I

THE FUNDAMENTALS

Before you learn how to build and run a team, you need to understand the reasons for creating a team in the first place, as well as what separates a true team from a collection of individuals.

Chapter 1

WHY A TEAM?

What's the number one reason real estate agents start a team? That's easy: money. They want more, and they want it now. Most team leaders (and aspiring team leaders) start out as rainmakers—high producers who have cracked the code on winning business in their market. That's probably where you are. You have plenty of clients, and you could get even more, but your capacity is maxed out. There just aren't enough hours in the day.

And more deals lead to more money, but also more pain. After all, real estate is a 24-7-365 business. You can't control when you receive offers or when a new house pops up on a buyer's phone, so you end up being on call all the time. You're on the road to burnout.

Forming a team will increase your capacity and take some of the burden off your shoulders. That means more business, therefore more money in your pocket. Right?

Wrong. We've seen it a thousand times. Agents who form teams are nearly always disappointed, and here's why: you've built your success by being a rainmaker . . . but that's not the same thing as being a team leader.

As a rainmaker, all you know is chasing and executing deals. Being a team leader requires different skills: building processes, investing in people, creating a shared culture, etc. Unfortunately, the real estate industry is not going to teach you those skills.

Here's what happens to most team leaders.

In your mind, expanding means replicating yourself. So you hire other agents, thinking everyone has a similar mindset and work ethic . . . and you're surprised when they don't demonstrate the level of commitment, effort, and skill you expected. Or perhaps you brought in young team members thinking you would mentor them, but they're so inexperienced that they don't even know the basics. You spend all your time teaching them how to do their jobs.

Either way, you quickly discover that no one can do anything as quickly or as well as you can. But the work has now multiplied, and you can't afford for every little thing to take twice as long. You can't stand to see the quality decline either.

So you try to do it all yourself.

This is where your team struggles. Everyone depends on you; they don't feel empowered or valued. They signed on with you because they knew you were a star and they were hoping your success would rub off on them. Instead, they feel frustrated and disengaged.

And they're not the only ones. You come to resent the very team you formed. They were supposed to take rote tasks off your hands so you could create more business, which would in turn benefit them. But as far as you can tell, they sit around waiting to be told what to do, even if you've explained it before. You're doing all the same work you did as a solo agent, plus you've got these additional mouths to feed.

End result? You burn out faster than ever. As we said earlier, if you want a recipe for working harder, making less, and having more stress, start a "team"—it works every time.

Case in point: In 2021, one of Steve's coaching clients had led a team that sold more than 300 homes totaling over $400 million. Sounds like massive success, right? But early in 2022, he admitted he wanted nothing more than a leave of absence.

He was burned out and pissed off. Concerned about his marriage, his family, and his sanity, he needed a break . . . but he couldn't take one. The guilt, the fear, the lack of trust, the idea that he would be setting a poor example for everyone, all combined to make him believe he just had to gut it out. Now was not the time to take a planned sabbatical, he told himself.

This is what happens when you don't do teams right. You have to pedal faster and faster to keep things going as profit margins shrink and the pressure to produce gets more and more intense.

Keep in mind that this was one of the highest-performing real estate teams in the country, and the founder is a smart, dedicated, hardworking person. But despite supposedly having a team, he still thought he had to do everything.

That's the number one trap team leaders all fall into. This book is about getting out of, and staying out of, that trap. The one thing you can't do is everything! If you try, you'll be overwhelmed and stretched like Gumby, trying to do too many things in too many places at the same time. Your efforts will fall far short of perfection, which only adds to the stress.

To get started, we'll help you understand the *real* reasons to create or join a team. It's not about instant gratification—if that's what you expect, you'll be sorely disappointed. A team is a long-term investment that will pay huge dividends not just for you but also for your clients, team members, vendors, and everyone else your team touches.

Reason #1: Compete More Effectively

Today, buyers spend just a few seconds on their phone deciding whether or not to view a listing. Making those seconds count requires a lot more work than it used to, more than any one person can do.

Before hitting the market, a house must be updated, staged, photographed, and marketed, all by specialists. It needs to look its best on a tiny cell phone screen to attract buyers. The process is far more front-loaded and involved today than it was just a few years ago. We often tell sellers, only half-jokingly, that they need to move out before they list if they want to get the highest and best offers for their home. (In some areas, this is common practice.)

As the listing agent, you are responsible for coordinating all of this, and it's imperative that you provide a top-quality experience from start to finish. After all, the easiest way to gain market share is through repeat clients and referrals, and to get those, you need to leave an outstanding impression. Quality control drives sales. To explain this more precisely, high quality won't guarantee high sales, but low quality will guarantee low sales. Great quality isn't the *only* thing you need, but you definitely need it.

Here, too, teams have an edge. Solo agents, especially those who have earned some success, often get so busy that they end up cutting corners or dropping the ball. A high-performing team, on the other hand, puts in place quality control measures that cannot be ignored even at the busiest times. Remember, selling lots of houses doesn't guarantee quality, but the reverse is true: if you weave quality into your team, sales will follow.

And quality follows reps. From his NFL days, Steve knows well that reps on the practice field lead to success on game day. In terms of refining techniques and tactics, a solo agent can't hope to compete against a team that's selling one hundred or more homes each year.

The more reps you do, the more knowledge you gain about your market. For example, Dana's team does three times as much business as any other team or agent in her market. This gives her team unmatched knowledge about what's happening with home values, market trends, and buyer and seller mentality, as well as appraisers, lenders, and tradespeople. A solo agent simply doesn't have the exposure to gather all that information.

Plus, selling lots of homes lets you build stronger relationships with your vendors. The more work you give them, the more valuable you are to them, and the higher they'll prioritize you in the busy times. They'll learn your way of doing things—and actually follow it—because it's well worth investing their time and effort in keeping you happy.

A high-performing team will provide a better client experience than a solo agent, even an excellent one, every time. Given the depth of knowledge and experience that a functional team brings to bear, even the best solo agents can't hope to compete.

Reason #2: Have a Life

As Steve has learned from decades of coaching, most agents are operating under the illusion that if they can just get more business, everything will be okay. With enough deals, enough income, they'll finally have the life they want.

It doesn't work like that. More transactions means more money, yes, but also more work. Eventually, the endless cycle of chasing and closing deals devours so much time and creates so much stress that any pleasure or sense of accomplishment from the additional income is erased. The entire purpose is defeated.

Real estate is a round-the-clock industry, full of variables you can't control. Your clients work all day, so much of your contact with them, in addition to the follow-up that comes from those interactions, takes place during evenings and weekends. Dana once had an offer come in at 11:00 p.m. on Christmas Eve. *You gotta be kidding me*, she thought. But that was when the buyer had the time to buy a house, so as any veteran agent knows, Dana tracked down her clients and reviewed the offer on Christmas Day. Ho ho ho, indeed.

There is nothing you can do to change this dynamic, and as your success increases, so do the demands. If you don't have a team, you don't even have the option of turning off your phone, let alone taking a leave of absence.

Having a team gives you control over your life. Together, you can give clients the 24-7-365 service they want without you—or any one team member—having to be on call all the time. Everyone on the team, including you, can have regular days off, take vacations, and deal with illnesses and emergencies without worrying that the business will fall apart.

These days, as leader of a high-performing team, Dana is grateful that those Christmas Eve client calls are a thing of the past. This is especially true when she's meeting with a successful solo agent who simply cannot get off his phone for ten minutes to catch up. Dana's phone, by contrast, has been forwarded to a team member, allowing Dana the freedom to see to other tasks, including her personal life. She's in control.

Reason #3: Have an Exit Strategy

For most agents, their last deal is their last paycheck. They spend thirty years breaking their back, but at the end they have nothing to show for it. They haven't built anything that can stand independent of them, that can be passed on or sold and continue to operate as a business. They built their business on personality, and you can't scale (or sell) personality. While this may not seem like an issue at the beginning of your career, as you get closer to the end, it becomes a huge problem.

Real estate is a low-barrier-to-entry business. That's one of its big draws, and a reason many career-changers are attracted to the industry. Unlike franchises, to take just one example, you don't need to make a major up-front investment to get started in real estate.

But this ease of entry has drawbacks. Because agents don't need a lot of capital to get started, they're not accustomed to the idea of investing time and money with a long-term payoff in mind. Rather than building for the long haul, including their eventual retirement or exit from the business, they spend their career on a hamster wheel, chasing the next deal.

Don't settle for that. If you're going to spend decades in this career, you should build equity that will pay you back later. A team makes this possible. It sets you up to monetize your years of effort through a succession plan, a sale, or an annuity.

But this sort of later payoff requires a shift in mindset, which is why we keep pointing out that most teams fail. You shouldn't form a team in hopes of doubling your revenue next month, or next quarter, or even next year. You must be prepared for gross revenue to dip at first, as the team gets up to speed. This patience pays off on the back end.

A team isn't about selling homes. It's about building a business. Those are two very different things. Ultimately, the business needs to operate without you. This reality doesn't always go over well in real estate, an industry dominated by big personalities with egos to match. But creating an organization that can thrive without you is how you not only say goodbye to those Christmas Eve phone calls, but also how you create a saleable asset.

Bonus Benefits

In addition to these three big reasons to form or join a real estate team, there are a couple of important additional benefits.

Camaraderie is one. Real estate can be a lonely business, especially at the top. A team provides support, friendship, and a sounding board. Being around other successful people who know their jobs and do them well is an uplifting experience. It brings about the best sort of competition, in which all team members strive to excel, not wanting to be the weak link in the chain. When a team is in sync—sharing core values, doing their jobs well, feeling grateful for the opportunity—it's a beautiful thing to behold. Whether you're the team leader or a member, being part of something bigger than yourself is deeply rewarding.

Another benefit of a high-performing team is that it creates better results for *all* stakeholders in the business, not just you. Team members and their families benefit from greater stability in pay and schedules. Clients know they're in good hands because of all the reps team members have put in to develop skills in their area of specialization. Vendors thrive on the steady stream of work your team provides, and they repay the favor with greater care and attention for your clients. Even brokerages benefit because many administrative tasks are handled at the team level—and because high sales volume boosts everybody's bottom line.

And at the end of the day, strong real estate teams that function as small businesses have the potential to transform the larger community's perception of the industry.

As we've noted, top agents tend to want instant gratification when they form a team. However, creating, developing, and maintaining a high-performing team requires a different mindset. When you're an independent contractor, your expenditures look like spending ("I could have devoted this marketing spend to a nice dinner"). When you're a business leader, you must view such expenses as investments that will pay you back over time—maybe a long time.

The investment is worth it. The more successful you become as a solo agent, the less time you have. This reduces your quality of life and forces you to cut corners with clients and other stakeholders. An effective team, on the other hand, lets you leverage your time, creating the type of synergy business schools love.

Just remember, building a team is a long-term investment. If you're not in it for the long haul, we don't recommend it. But if you're truly ready to make the commitment, the first thing to consider is what makes a high-performing team. We'll explore this next.

Chapter 2

WHAT IS A TEAM?

As we've said, most real estate "teams" are teams in name only. This is true even of the ones that appear to be successful. We've met with many teams that rank in the top 1 percent of production in markets across the country, with volumes often topping $300 million a year . . . and yet, when you look behind the curtain, it's a shit show.

The team leaders complain that they're expected to do everything. Why did they form a team, they ask, if all the marketing, business development, and administrative tasks were going to end up in their lap? Even though their teams might be doing extraordinarily well according to typical industry metrics, every team member is stressed and unhappy, including the leader.

To top it all off, when we examine those businesses closely, we find that productivity isn't so high after all. If these teams were performing to their potential, their revenues could be double or even triple what they actually are.

Where do things go haywire?

It all starts with a simple problem: no one understands what it means to be a team. They don't know what that looks like or how it's different from just working in the same office under the same boss.

It's different because a high-functioning real estate team has the right structure, the right processes, and the right people, doing the right things, the right way, at the right time—consistently.

That's a lot of "rights." They don't happen by default or magic; they happen through four key transformations. This chapter will give you a bird's-eye view of each one and how it contributes to the making of a true team.

Leadership

You can't have a team without a leader.

Sure, sometimes a small group of people can function okay for a while by consensus alone. However, when it comes to making tough choices (and it always does come to that, eventually) someone has to be the final authority. Without a leader, even a small group can't work effectively toward a common goal over the long term.

Make no mistake: the bigger your team gets, the more leading you'll have to do. Grow enough, and it will become impossible to be the star player *and* the coach. Just look to the world of sports, where this strategy virtually always fails. You have to go back to basketball legend Bill Russell, in the 1960s, to find a successful player–coach in the top leagues.

There's a reason for that. The skills it takes to perform on the field are fundamentally different from those required to lead a team. Even if one athlete can master both sets of skills, they can't possibly perform both roles at the same time. There's just too much to do and not enough time or mental bandwidth.

The same goes for real estate. Star agents typically start teams without any idea what it takes to be a leader. After all, they built their success in a brutally competitive, individualistic, me-first industry. They've got the skills to win listings and negotiate favorable deals, but unfortunately, that's not what it takes to manage and satisfy a diverse group of professionals.

That's why we see so many agents form a team, learn firsthand the challenges involved, and then change their minds. They think they're going to be the quarterback *and* the coach, but it just doesn't work that way. By starting a team, you are committing to a fundamental change in your role. The more people you hire, the more leading you'll need to do, until pretty soon that's your whole job.

In the next chapter, you'll learn exactly what that new job looks like. Fair warning: doing it well means saying goodbye to your ego. Your business is not about only you anymore. It's also about your *team*.

Strategy

The foundation of any team is a shared aim and plan of attack.

When Steve was playing for the Dolphins, that aim was a Super Bowl ring. Money was nice, and wins were great, but only a Super Bowl win could show that they were the best in the world, and that was always the ultimate goal. One person could never get that ring alone; for anyone to get it, *everyone* had to get it. The whole team had to be working toward the same thing, 100 percent of the time.

They also had to agree on how to get there. There wasn't enough time in the day to do everything well—to train every muscle, every skill, every possible play to perfection. The coaches had to make choices about what to focus on and what to let go to give the team the best chance of success. There could be only one unified approach, or the team would never reach their goal.

The same goes for your team. This is a notoriously difficult notion for real estate agents, who are so often mired in an independent-contractor mindset. But you're not independent anymore. You and your team members all depend on each other for success because you're trying to achieve something no single member (including you) could do on their own. You're trying to sell more and have a better quality of life than you ever could by yourself. Otherwise, why form a team at all?

As team leader, it's up to you to decide what the team is aiming for and how you're going to get there. What geographic areas will you focus on? What types of properties and clients? What price points? And within that niche, what do you hope to achieve?

Whatever you decide your team's equivalent to the Super Bowl ring is, you need to declare it, articulate it, and gain alignment on it from all team members. For example, when we conceived of this book project, one of our first group activities was to create a document, appropriately called our North Star, to help us align on our shared goals. We each vocalized our vision for the book and came to a consensus on exactly what it would be about, who it would be for, how it would sound, and what we hoped to achieve with it. Throughout the writing process, we referred back to our North Star for guidance anytime our focus threatened to wander.

Strategic alignment is the foundation of teamwork: everyone has to know what you're doing and why you're doing it. Only then can you begin working together to achieve your goals.

Organization

A team is a business first and foremost, and businesses have structure: defined roles and processes that make the work more predictable and efficient.

While this may sound obvious, it's a major roadblock for most team leaders. As a solo agent, you probably didn't have much in the way of processes. If you were anything like most agents, you worked reactively, responding to whatever opportunities crossed your path and whatever clients demanded of you from moment to moment. You counted on your brokerage to handle administrative processes, so you never had to pay attention to anything other than chasing and closing the next deal.

That might have been enough to bring you success on your own, but it becomes total chaos when other people come on board. Without clearly delineated responsibilities and ways of doing things, your team members will fall back into the comfort zone of solo-agent behavior. They'll compete with each other and try to do everything themselves instead of collaborating and allowing specialists to support them.

In that situation, what value do your agents get from being on a team? Not much. Pretty soon, they'll start to think—perhaps correctly—that they'd be better off on their own, and they'll leave.

And what about your administrators and back-office specialists? They'll feel ignored and frustrated that their talents are going to waste, and they'll get tired of being treated like second-class citizens by agents who are obsessed with sales and blind to operations. Before long, they'll get fed up and leave too.

To avoid this outcome, everyone needs a clear role that allows them to play to their strengths.

Solo agents are accustomed to doing everything themselves, but that's not the best use of their time. Their strengths are in serving clients, and that's where they should spend as much time as possible. As your team grows, you should take more and more responsibilities off their plates and give them to others who specialize in those areas—people like assistants, administrators, marketers, accountants, and more.

The more each person can focus on their strengths, the more effective the whole team can be. This can happen only when each person has a clear part to play and understands how their role interacts with all the other roles on the team. On the football field, Steve recalls, the more he understood what everyone else was doing and trusted that they would do it, the better he could play his own position. It freed him up to focus on his job without worrying about covering for someone else.

In addition to clear roles, you need defined processes: specific ways your team does the tasks that make the business run. We're talking tools, procedures, checklists, guidelines—all the things that make the work consistent and reliable.

When you were on your own, you probably developed your way of doing things, and you probably never bothered to write it down because it was all right there in your head. Sure, once in a while you would mix up the order a little or accidentally miss a step (oops), but you could cover those mistakes. You never had to explain to anyone how or why you did things the way you did.

Now you do. If everyone on your team does things their own way, the result will be confusion, dropped balls, and unhappy clients—actually, unhappy everyone. Nobody wants to be left wondering what they're supposed to do or what they should expect from their teammates. That leads to wasted time, unnecessary conflict, and subpar work quality. To keep the gears of your business turning smoothly—and to optimize them over time—you need formal processes that are written down and shared with the whole team.

This applies throughout the entire business. It's not just about back-office functions like payroll, recordkeeping, and compliance. The client-facing side (marketing, sales, client service, etc.) needs structure too. For many single agents, their name on the sign and occasional mailers are all the marketing they've ever known. That won't cut it when you're trying to build a genuine business that will someday be able to operate without you.

You may have been "successful" in the past without worrying about this stuff, but don't let that fool you. At the beginning of this chapter, we told you about several $300 million–plus teams that were massively underperforming their potential. How did we know that was true? Because their marketing and business development efforts were totally disorganized. If they could do over $300 million in sales that way, how much more could they achieve with streamlined, replicable, measurable processes?

Culture

On a real team, everyone is in it together.

It's not just about having a shared aim—that's strategy. Culture is about how team members view and treat each other. A great team fosters a culture of camaraderie, where people support and appreciate each other as they work toward their shared goals.

This is *not* the natural state of affairs among real estate agents. In general, people will die for their autonomy—anything that undermines their perceived control over their lives is viewed as a threat.[1] In real estate, that dynamic is amplified. It's an individualistic industry where most people work independently, which tends to attract those who value their autonomy the most. This is a self-reinforcing dynamic that leads most agents to adopt a me-first mentality that pits them against other agents. Even within a team, competition for the best leads and the most sales can be fierce—and the winners often lord their prowess over everyone else.

No team can function that way. Have you ever seen a basketball or soccer game where every single person is trying to be the one who puts the ball in the net? It's not pretty. Each player tries to keep the ball for themselves, even when passing, blocking, or doing something else would give the team a better chance to score.

1 This is a core teaching of Chris Voss, the noted negotiation expert and co-author with Steve Shull on *The Full Fee Agent*.

Opportunity after opportunity gets ignored or wasted because of this egocentric attitude.

This recently happened to one of Steve's coaching clients. She leads a team in New York City, where buyers of co-ops must be approved by boards that are notoriously picky. One of her agents, a productive but independent-minded person, had two buyer clients who put in offers on co-op properties . . . and *both* got rejected, wrecking two extremely lucrative deals.

The real problem was that the agent never asked for help. If the team leader had known the deals were falling apart, she probably could have helped save them. But the agent didn't think about that—she just wanted to win on her own and be the hero. That's the solo agent way.

As a leader, it's your job to show your team a different way.

That means celebrating the team as a whole and showing appreciation for every single role. This alone is a major attitude shift. Real estate isn't a what-have-you-done-for-me-lately industry; it's more of a what-can-you-do-for-me-in-the-next-twenty-minutes industry. It's an outgrowth of the independent-contractor mindset, in which agents constantly chase transactions. They're always in a screaming hurry to check off any boxes that will bring them closer to the closing.

As a business built for the long haul, a team functions differently. The person in the office researching demographic trends in your market isn't going to make anyone rich in the next twenty minutes. Neither is the person updating your website, or the one peppering you with forms to ensure compliance. But each of those team members is contributing in their own way, and all have to receive the same respect the hotshot agents get. You have to be the one to demonstrate that every role is recognized and valued—and the one to correct teammates when they behave otherwise.

Nurturing team culture also means uplifting the people around you. Your team will be looking to you to set an upbeat, can-do tone. Fortunately, top agents who become team leaders tend to be outgoing types who enjoy being around others and are naturally cheerful. There are exceptions, and that's okay; nobody is trying to dictate what your personality should be. But with leadership comes responsibilities, and keeping the troops encouraged and motivated is one of them. This can be a challenge when business is rough or your personal life gets rocky, but remember that your people take their cues from you—your attitude is contagious whether you like it or not.

Of course, choosing the right people and teaching them how to be part of your team is also a huge part of building team culture. You need people who *want* to be part of a cooperative team and are ready to set their ego aside. To get the benefit of resources and support that solo agents never have, they have to give up the freedom of doing things whenever and however they want.

On a team, what each person does—or fails to do—affects everyone else. Single agents can get away with delays and mistakes by working harder tomorrow. But on a team, there's a ripple effect. When one person doesn't complete their tasks, they make life harder and less profitable for everyone. Everyone on the team needs to understand and respect that interdependence. The team is only as strong as its weakest link, so everyone needs to have each other's backs, no matter what.

Teams work only when they create value for everyone. Everyone on the team, including you, should be getting better results than they would on their own. Remember, if two plus two doesn't equal at least five, everybody's time is being wasted.

That's exactly what's happening in those "teams" that are really just loose collections of individual agents. Everyone is doing their own thing, duplicating efforts, and competing with one another—all because they don't understand what a team really is.

As you've just learned, a true team has four things:

- **Leadership**: One person who is the ultimate authority and holder of responsibility
- **Strategy**: A shared aim and plan for how to reach it
- **Organization**: Clear roles and processes to structure and optimize the work
- **Culture**: A shared belief that you're all in it together, and everyone's effort matters

Just understanding what teams are and why you should (or shouldn't) start one is part of your transformation from solo agent to team leader. Misconceptions about these things are the most common reason teams fail, and we definitely don't want that for you.

But there's more to this transformation, as you'll see in the next chapter. You've already seen hints of how a leader's job is different from an alpha agent's job. Now, it's time to learn exactly what those differences are and decide whether you want to take them on.

PART II

PRE-SEASON PLANNING

This is when you make big, fundamental decisions to put your house in order before things get hectic. That includes shifting from a solo agent to a team-leader mindset, developing your team culture and brand, deciding your team structure, and defining your business strategy.

Chapter 3

BECOMING A TEAM LEADER

Recently, Dana was with a group of extremely high-performing agents at a real estate conference. One woman complained bitterly that her team leader was making the team miserable. He micromanaged. He made all the decisions. He even tried to hide the fact that his team members did a lion's share of the work, as he wanted to be seen as the superhero and the one that could do it all.

None of the agents felt they got any trust, credibility, or credit from their leader. He was a nice person, and they knew he just wanted the business to thrive. But how could it when his actions left his team perpetually frustrated and disengaged?

This is what happens when a team "leader" never develops a leadership mindset.

It's all too common in real estate. After all, the industry attracts a certain type of person. Agents value their independence; they don't like to be told what to do and when to do it. They love the glory and sense of accomplishment that comes with achieving things on their own.

But here's the rub: that me-focused orientation is counterproductive when it comes to building and running a team. If you keep trying to do everything yourself, everyone else becomes dependent on you. They have to wait on you to make decisions, tell them what to do, and approve their every move. Even with a small team, this quickly stretches you beyond your capacity and pushes you toward burnout.

It's true that great teams are interdependent, but the leader can't be the bottleneck. To understand why, start with the end in mind. Your goal is to build a business that can give you greater profits *and* your life back. You can't do it all by yourself, so somewhere along the way, you need to develop the ability to empower other people.

The time to start is now. Too many teams crash and burn while the leader keeps grinding away, promising to turn over the reins as soon as a few more transactions are in the books. This is a surefire recipe for team leader burnout, team member frustration, and eventual failure.

Bottom line: you can't do everything.

This might sound obvious, but it's the one idea that trips up virtually every team leader in real estate. To truly understand and apply it, you have to transform four core beliefs around your role as you go from solo agent to team leader. Those four beliefs are what you'll learn in this chapter. They are the bedrock of everything else you'll learn in this book—none of the rest will work unless you take this first step.

And you won't find this step in any other real estate training. Don't go looking to other real estate team leaders for help on this—they haven't mastered it any better than you have. Nothing in this industry teaches you how to make the transformation from rainmaker to team leader.

That's why we're going back to the very basics. It's not crazy—it's just good coaching practice. Legendary football coach Vince

Lombardi used to open each training camp by saying, "Gentleman, this is a football." Bud Grant, another NFL legend, had the Minnesota Vikings practice standing for the national anthem. And John Wooden, the great basketball coach, taught players how to put on their socks and lace their shoes.

Great fundamentals make all the difference.

Your Team Is Your Client

***Mindset shift**: The buyer/seller is my client → the team member is my client*

Once you form a team, buyers and sellers are no longer your only clients. Your team members are also clients.

This fundamental change in thinking does not come easy to agents reared in the highly competitive, me-focused world of real estate. But it's a necessary shift; everything else hinges on it.

Your job isn't only to buy and sell houses anymore. It's also to *empower your team* to do that. You want *them* to hit targets, to get accolades, to hear other agents in the brokerage whistle in admiration when their quarterly numbers are announced. You want clients trusting *them*, seeking their advice, referring them to others, sending them thank-you notes and flowers.

That's how you know you're building equity. The less your team members depend on you to generate leads and shepherd deals, the more valuable your business is, because it can operate without you. The more you hang on to your old role of making sales, the more you hold back this positive development. As Dana puts it, she'll know her team is truly valuable when she herself brings in *none* of the business.

Nobody says this sea change will be easy. Many leaders are afraid of giving up their client relationships. It's understandable—those relationships are often deeply personal and a source of joy. It's difficult to entrust them to another person.

But you have to shift your thinking now that you're a leader. It's time to find new joy in the growth of your team members. Dana doesn't get as many thank-you bouquets as she used to—but her team members sure do, and client referrals mention their names alongside Dana's. This is a source of pleasure and pride, as Dana knows she helped put these team members in a position to succeed.

Don't let ego get in the way of supporting and celebrating your team. Some team leaders are so eager to keep the spotlight on themselves that they try to hide their agents and pretend they're not a team at all. You need to do the opposite: show off your team members. Help them shine. Talk to prospects and clients about "my team" and "us," not "me."

This will gratify them on a personal level, boost their professional profile, and most importantly, make your brand bigger than just you. That's a huge part of building a business that runs perfectly well without you. We're not asking you to give up your ego or your ambition—after all, they are what put you in a position to be a team-builder in the first place. Rather, reframe your ego, broadening it to include your entire team.

Now it's time to ask yourself a key question: Will you be happy if your job is catering to team members instead of clients? Can you get as much satisfaction from their success as from closing deals yourself?

There's no wrong answer here—but if your reply is no, leading a team is not for you.

You Have to Let Go

Mindset shift: *I can do everything better myself →*
I trust my team to do their jobs

Here's the team leader paradox, one we've seen over and over again. You start a team because you can't do everything. Your success as an individual agent has made you so busy that you need help with tasks that are important, but which don't appeal to you or prevent you from spending sufficient time with clients.

Maybe it's accounting that slips through the cracks—goodness knows you've got better things to do than save receipts and track your mileage. Maybe you've had so many referrals calling (a great problem to have!) that you haven't kept up with demographic trends in your market. Or maybe you're not getting around to such simple-but-important chores as ordering sufficient Open House signs.

So you create a team. Let others handle the mundane jobs, the "administrivia," while you do the important work: one-on-one time with clients, winning listings, closing deals.

But once you've formed that team, you find out that (surprise!) not everybody is a superstar. Most of the time, your team members don't know what to do unless you spell it out for them. Plus, every task takes them twice as long as it took you, and the result is half as good. So you just do it yourself. After all, you don't have time to wait, and you don't want poor-quality work to damage your reputation.

Now, you have all the responsibilities and challenges of a team . . . and none of the benefits. You're working harder than ever while your team members are bored, frustrated, and not improving their skills.

Virtually every real estate team leader does this to some degree. Just as superstar athletes seldom make good coaches because their sport comes to them so easily, alpha agents tend to be blinded by their own abilities. They don't understand why others can't do what they've been doing, so they get annoyed. It's understandable . . . but it's also the wrong approach.

Just because you're the best at a given task doesn't mean you should do it. As team leader, you should be focused on the activities that generate the most value, the ones that *only* you can do: strategy, planning, and management. Your team should be taking everything else off your plate.

If you're not happy with how fast or how well they're doing that work, *train them to do it better*. Rather than wanting them to be more like you, figure out what their best effort looks like and coach them up. Give them as many opportunities to practice as possible—that's the only way they'll improve. It takes a little extra time at first, but it saves you *much* more in the long run.

To take one common example, many team leads struggle to hand off business to their agents. They may be convinced that clients want them and not anyone else. Or perhaps they don't trust their agents to handle the relationships and transactions in a way that meets their standards.

Again, this hesitance is understandable. After all, the client experience depends on the agent more than anyone, and there's no denying that an inexperienced agent may struggle to meet your standards. Nevertheless, you have to give them a chance to try.

You also have to let them learn to manage their own work. At a recent industry event, one team leader commented to Dana, "I don't know how you find the time to get your work done. It takes me two hours a day just to make up everybody's to-do list." She was spending 25 percent of a full-time work week just telling her people what to do, when they should be able to figure that out for themselves. When the goals, roles, and processes are clear, and people have been taught to do their jobs, they don't need their team leader to hold their hand.

In the end, your team can't own their responsibilities until *you* let those responsibilities go. Train them up front, offer guidance and support, then trust them to do their job. When people arrive at a place where they're able to do things on their own, you have to let them.

Dana knows firsthand how hard this is to learn. For years, she allowed herself to wear the hat of chief shit-picker-upper, always running around cleaning up everyone's messes. And guess what? Despite her best efforts, the problems didn't disappear. Why? Because her team members weren't learning how to solve or prevent them on their own. This wasn't her team's fault. It was her fault.

But as Dana mastered team leadership, that changed. Recently, when interest rate hikes caused a major upheaval in real estate, she was on vacation, thousands of miles from home. What did she do? She continued to enjoy her vacation. Clients were nervous and deals were in danger of falling apart, but Dana's agents didn't need her to rescue them. All they needed was some strategic advice, which she gladly provided on a conference call with the whole team.

This kind of trust has to be earned, but it won't happen if you don't give people the opportunity. Set your team up for success by giving them a foundation of clear processes, adequate training, and ongoing support—otherwise they'll fail, which will further erode your trust. When they're ready, *let go*. Let them do their jobs.

Are you prepared to leave your ego at the door? Are you willing to give up control and trust others? If not, don't try to lead a team.

The Buck Stops with You

Mindset shift: *I'm looking out for myself →*
I'm responsible for my entire team

Becoming a team lead is a massive hike in responsibility. Where once you had to look out only for yourself, you're now responsible for the livelihoods of others.

It's not just about providing a paycheck. You're also the source of opportunities, training, and support. They look to you for reasons and solutions when the market turns rough. They're counting on you to maintain the health of the business so it can thrive and continue to support everyone over the long term, even when times are tough.

This requires something that agents rarely bother with: investment. Most solo agents think of every expense as a dollar coming out of their own pocket. They want to take home as much money as possible, so they keep those expenses at the bare minimum, reluctant to spend money on anything that's not strictly necessary for the immediate function of the business. Many agents don't even have any personal savings for themselves, let alone business savings.

That's not an option when you're leading a team. Now, you have an obligation to reinvest in the business so it can continue to operate in the long run. That means you'll have to spend some money up front to build infrastructure, hire people, train them, and market your brand. It almost always takes time—months or even years—to see returns on those investments.

In addition to being responsible for your team members' livelihoods, you're also responsible for their actions. That's right—you're legally liable for what they say and do. So yes, make sure you've got business liability insurance, but more importantly, invest time and energy into building effective training and quality-control processes. That will help you prevent mistakes or catch them early, before they lead to lawsuits.

On top of all that (as if that wasn't enough responsibility already), you also set the ultimate example of how to think, speak, and act in your team. This level of power and influence is not to be taken lightly. It sets the tone for your entire team culture because people *will* follow your lead.

So where are you leading them? Are you showing them how to make everyone feel welcome and valued? Are you demonstrating how to listen with an open mind and convey your ideas with respect and consideration for others? Or are you practicing some behaviors you'd rather they *not* emulate? You don't have to be perfect—just be aware that you're being watched. Your behavior is the ultimate indicator of what's acceptable and what's not in your team.

These are serious burdens to bear. Are you prepared to take responsibility for other people's livelihoods and actions? Are you financially ready and willing to invest in your team without an immediate return? Are you confident that you can lead by example when it comes to behavior and culture? If not, you're not ready to lead a team.

Your Job Is to Think Ahead

Mindset shift: *I react to client needs →*
I proactively plan for team needs

Most solo agents spend all day, every day reacting to clients' needs.

A day in your solo-agent life probably includes activities like listing appointments, closings, open houses, negotiating, meeting inspectors, and of course, responding to client calls. Your whole day is filled with these urgent things that demand your attention right away. Does this sound familiar?

These are all vital aspects of the business, of course. However, that list probably includes several activities that don't play to your strengths and aren't the ideal use of your time. And that never-ending cycle of urgency means you rarely, if ever, step back from the day-to-day and think about the future. When the minutiae of your current deals consume your days (and evenings and weekends), there's no time to plan ahead.

A team leader has to do the opposite. It's no longer your job to make sales and shepherd deals. Your job is to position your team members in the right place, doing the right things, in the right way, for the good of the business. Compare the following partial list of daily activities for a team leader to the reactive tasks noted above:

- Communicating and reinforcing roles, responsibilities, values, process, and expectations
- Watching and analyzing the market in order to develop the team strategy
- Building and promoting the team brand
- Reviewing performance data and searching for opportunities to improve
- Nurturing relationships with leads and past clients
- Making decisions about hiring, promoting, and firing

These are *proactive* responsibilities that a real estate team leader shares with the CEO of any small business—or large business, for that matter. This is a completely different job from a solo agent, requiring a proactive mindset and discipline.

For example, one of the most important leadership tasks Dana does every week is developing and delivering the team's message, i.e., what's happening in the market and how they're going to talk about it to their clients. She does market research, takes a position, and holds a weekly meeting with all her agents to get aligned on it. They get clear answers on how they should be addressing clients' concerns, and she gets reassurance that her agents are presenting a united front. Thanks to her strategic work, every agent on her team talks just like Dana, which gives her a strong brand and consistently high quality.

That's the power of thinking ahead. Are you prepared to shift from a reactive to a proactive approach? Are you willing to trade client-focused work for team-focused work? If not, leading a team isn't for you.

—

The real estate industry has long been a home for self-starters—determined, hardworking people who want to set their own schedules and succeed on their own terms. This meritocratic individualism is one of the things we love about the business. But transitioning from hard-charging solo agent to team leader requires a different set of skills and attitudes, not all of which come naturally to rainmaker agents.

If you've read this far and are still determined to form or join a team—to go from *me* to *we*—congratulations! The next big step to take is to decide exactly who that *we* is—not in terms of your personnel, but in terms of your identity as a team. Who are you and what do you stand for? Your culture and brand will answer that question.

Chapter 4

CULTURE AND BRAND

Picture these situations.

Scenario #1: It's a tough market, with prices dropping dramatically from recent highs. Other agents are quoting sellers inflated prices—prices from three months ago, not today—just to get listings.

You don't do that. Instead, you explain the market shift to sellers and inform them they probably can't hope to match recent comps.

Why do you make this decision, which in the short run will cost you listings? Because you value open and honest communication. You also value creating amazing experiences, and you know that quoting an inflated price only to reduce it later creates a terrible experience for the seller.

Scenario #2: One of your team members visits a lead and comes back recommending that you pass on the listing. They explain their reasoning, which is sound. The house is suffering from long-term neglect, or the sellers are unpleasant to the point of nastiness, or something about the situation just seems off.

You let the opportunity go, even though it stings to do so.

Why are you willing to watch business walk away? Because you value trust in your team. You believe in the agent and trust that they're making the right call.

Scenario #3: You're having a terrible week, but one of your agents is hitting it out of the park. Putting your bad mood and your competitiveness aside, you congratulate them on their achievements.

Why? Because you value celebrating success. Any member's success equates to success for the entire team. You may be having a rough week, but you can find joy in your teammate's achievement.

In each of these scenarios, you face a choice about how to behave.

There isn't always a single correct answer. After all, in Scenario #1, it could be argued that winning a listing, no matter how you do it, is the best move not only for your team but for the seller. But the answer you *do* choose depends on and reinforces team culture and brand.

Culture is what creates your team identity internally. *Brand* is what communicates it externally.

This identity is the definition of who you are and how you do business. It's what bonds the team together and makes it unique. It's how you attract the right people to you—not just team members but also partners and clients.

Most importantly, your culture guides your thinking and actions day-to-day. When you or your team members aren't sure which course of action to take, culture and brand will guide you, ensuring consistency over time and across the team.

Core Values and Principles

The first step in defining your culture is to identify your team's core values. Values are what you care about, what you prioritize, what you demand of yourselves and each other.

Not everyone on your team will share all the same values, to be sure. But you should be able to create a clear, curated list that everyone can get on board with. "Clear" means everyone understands what the words truly mean, in terms of actions and behaviors. "Curated" means the list is focused on truly top priorities.

Identifying your core values needs to be a team exercise. This is the only way to get buy-in from team members and come up with a meaningful list. That said, you can't expect to gain 100 percent agreement from everyone on every value, and you can't prioritize *everything*. Trying to do that will water down your list until it means nothing and has no power. So the process of crafting your team's values will require some iteration and some give-and-take from everyone.

When Dana first took on this task, she asked each person on her team to come up with ten suggestions on their own. Then they all came together, with Dana's operations specialist facilitating the conversation. It started with pooling and sorting all the suggestions to find common themes. For example, almost everyone said something about family, so of course that made it onto the list. Other concepts that often came up included positivity, integrity, and trust.

But what does it *mean* to value family, or any of these things? It's not enough to list a bunch of abstract ideas. The next step is to define what they mean in terms of *specific behavior and actions.*

This is no time for feel-good cliches or gray areas that are open to interpretation. That only leads to misunderstandings, conflict, and chaos. Without a shared understanding of how to *act* on the core values, everybody will be doing their own dance steps. To keep the team marching as one and hold them accountable for living the values, you've got to come to an explicit agreement on what that looks like.

For example, after some discussion, Dana's team agreed that valuing family means being there for their families in the important moments. That includes both planned events, like birthdays, as well as unexpected ones, like illnesses. For that to be possible, team members have to be willing to help each other out in those moments. When one agent needs to put their family above work, the others will cover for them, but they have to do the same for their teammates in return.

Now, that paragraph-long explanation is very clear, but not very concise. If you want to keep the team values at the top of everyone's mind, they need to be easy to remember, and ideally, easy to put on a wall or a desk. That means you need a phrase that's short and punchy but still captures the essential meaning of the behaviors you've agreed on as a team. For family, Dana's team settled on the words, "Family first."

In addition to family, many team members suggested values related to education and professional development. Discussion helped narrow this broad concept down: team members should not only seek to increase their knowledge and expertise but also share it across the team. Those who want to take a course or gain a certification are given the time and space to do so, and when someone has valuable information about a client, a market, a listing, a competitor, or anything else that might benefit the team, they should speak up. This value became "Seek and share knowledge."

Another common value was positivity. The team agreed that they should all bring a positive attitude to work and aim to create positive experiences for others, both teammates and clients, even when doing so isn't easy. This became "Choose positive"—notice how just adding one word makes this value actionable rather than vague. There's always a choice about what kind of energy or outlook to bring to a situation, and the team has agreed on which is the right answer.

That's the power of carefully crafted values. The words convey a clear meaning to every team member, and because everyone was involved in the process, the values actually drive their behavior.

When you take on this challenge, keep in mind that it's not an intellectual exercise. It's about the heart more than the head. For Dana's team, several one- to two-hour sessions were required to come up with final options and vote on them. You can see the results here:

A great deal of hard work goes into this exercise, but it will pay off in spades. Because they truly believe in their core values, and because Dana makes it a point to keep the list front and center, team members refer to their values daily in conversation. "Sorry, gotta step out a bit early—family first," someone might say. Or, "It's been a tough week, but hey—choose positive." Or, "Seek and share knowledge—I learned something interesting yesterday."

Even though Dana's team values are strong, there's only so much that can be said in so few words. They can't capture detailed, specific expectations about team members' behavior, not in a way that can be used to train or evaluate them.

That's what the "core principles" are for. This is a much longer list that spells out exactly how an effective team member behaves, regardless of their specific job. For example, here's the first core principle, "Communicating with Impact":

- Communicate weekly with Team Lead
- Copy Team Lead on all contractual documents, offers made, and negotiations
- Meet and partner with team members as needed
- Routinely communicate, educate, and share within the team
- Respond in a timely manner to client, vendor, and team requests
- Own the client relationship
- Introduce new clients to Team Lead and other appropriate team members
- Obtain new business and send data to executive assistant to record in lead tracker

As you can see, the core principles are fairly extensive. This level of specificity lets team members know exactly what is expected of them. Few teams take this crucial additional step, but it's an incredibly useful one. These principles should be part of job descriptions, contracts, and performance evaluation forms—that's how you hold everyone accountable for living up to them.

Dana wrote the first draft of these principles herself, then asked all team members for input before finalizing them. She also consulted with an HR attorney to make sure the principles complied with labor laws for independent contractors. That's important—the principles make expectations clear without crossing any legal lines. After all, Dana can't forbid agents from getting tipsy at a local restaurant, standing on a table, and belting out a song. She can, however, remind them that they represent the brand at all times.

The principles also provide a standard by which to evaluate not only individual members, but the team as a whole: Are they living up to their values? That's a question the team asks itself every year, and they look to the principles to help keep themselves on track.

Living the Culture

Many teams have their values, mission, or vision written down somewhere, but few use them. Oh, they may be posted on the team website or printed in the handbook, but no one is actually thinking about them. Team members couldn't tell you what the team values or vision were if you quizzed them, and even the leader doesn't think about them often. Everybody's too busy chasing that next deal.

That's a problem because culture is powerful. It guides members' behavior in both obvious and subtle ways, whether people realize it or not. If your team isn't on the same page about their culture, conflict and confusion will follow. What kind of behavior is acceptable? What's the right course of action in a given situation? Who's a good fit for the team, and who isn't?

To keep people aligned on questions like these, you have to make culture an explicit part of everyday life in your team, not an abstraction they can ignore. Display key pieces of it—such as your values—where your team sees it every day, like on the walls or on their desks. Talk about it in team meetings. Periodically reflect on it and make revisions.

For example, Dana's team has goals related to each value, and they evaluate themselves against those goals each quarter. Once a year, Dana asks people to pick their favorite core value and share what it means to them. She also asks the team to revisit the core principles and suggest updates and improvements.

Another important step is to take your culture public. Talk about it in your marketing materials, like your website and brochures; it should be a strong selling point. Dana calls her public statement of culture the team's "ethos" (see below), although you could call it a philosophy, mission statement, or whatever you want. What matters is that clients, prospects, and partners who see this summary immediately understand what the team is all about.

DANA GREEN TEAM ETHOS

We believe in long-term impact—that knowledge is power, design is critical, and reputation is everything. We hold the big picture for our clients, which guides our thinking and actions.

We strive for meaningful real estate outcomes by maintaining a consistent focus on process, execution, and a positive outlook. We mark our communities with deep relationships and outcomes that benefit everyone, not just our business. Every one of us plays a part to manifest our greatest collective potential, in work and in life.

Remember, your team culture is not what you *should be* or *wish you were*. It's what you *are* and what you *do*. So once you develop a culture, don't simply check a box and move on to the next to-do. Try it on. Wear it around for a while. Make sure it really fits.

And watch out for those who would undermine it. Every person on your team is either strengthening the culture or weakening it, and as the saying goes, one enemy inside the tent is worth a thousand outside it. One toxic person who refuses to get on board can seriously damage your team, both in terms of productivity and quality of life. If they're not part of the solution, they're part of the problem, and they have to go.

Note that even something as unpleasant as firing a team member has an upside: it illustrates the loopholes and gaps in your processes. That person isn't a bad human being—you just need to adjust your hiring process so it's easier to judge who will be a good cultural fit and who won't. As Dana always says, blame the process, not the person (more on that in Chapter 7).

Ultimately, nurturing the culture is the team leader's job—it ends with everyone, but it starts with you.

Brand Identity

Once you've clarified your internal culture, you can build a strong brand—that is, the public face of your team culture. Brand identity encompasses your entire public appearance, from the things you say and the images you show down to the fonts, colors, and designs you use. All this should embody and reflect your culture. This is how you share with the world who you are, what you value, and why you're different.

It's also how you make the team bigger than just your personality. Remember, a strong team is a business; you're building it to transcend and outlast you. Your brand is part of that effort.

Does this sound like a major undertaking? It is! Or should be. The truth is, most teams don't go through any type of formal brand development process.

That's a mistake. Without deliberate decisions and clear guidelines, you end up with a "brand" that's just plain confusing. Every marketing asset—the website, social media, ads, and other printed materials—gets created on the fly, with no overarching guideposts, often by different people who aren't communicating with each other. As a result, each item looks and sounds a little different—and that's no way to make a memorable impression.

Does this sound familiar? It's extremely common. Jonathan has performed dozens of marketing audits, and he often finds that teams have three or four slightly different looks going at once. That's not a true brand at all; it's a mishmash. And when the team brand isn't strong, each agent will want to market themselves with their own name and look, further diluting the brand.

In today's world, that's not going to cut it. People need to find your team, to *recognize* your team, online. They should feel a connection with your team before anybody ever gets on the phone with them, through repeated exposure to consistent brand messaging. And they should trust that your team knows how to market their house—not likely if it looks like you don't even know how to market yourselves.

Another common branding pitfall is focusing on the team leader over the team. Your brand isn't all about you anymore. In fact, the more it revolves around you, the less valuable it is—once again, the whole idea here is to build something that can thrive *without* you one day. But many team leaders continue to use "I" instead of "we" and put their solo headshot everywhere.

What does that tell people about your team? Nothing. In fact, it leaves the distinct impression that they don't matter. When people call, they're going to want to work with you personally, not some anonymous team they know nothing about. Your team members will get the message, too, and soon they'll start to wonder if they wouldn't be better off on their own.

Even if the team was your brainchild, and even if you're bringing in the lion's share of the volume (for now), you'll enjoy far more long-term success if you build the brand around the team, not merely yourself. Dana is a stickler for this. Because of state law, her name has to be in the company name, but she always talks about the Dana Green *Team*, not herself. Everything is "we," never "I." During a recent photo shoot, the photographer wanted to place her in the front of each shot, but she insisted on being in the middle instead, to show they are all peers.

By building a team-based brand, you are creating value for your team members—a reason for them to stick around. They don't have to do all the work of creating their own brand and building a reputation. They can use the team brand, which is both ready-made and gives them a fair share of the limelight by positioning them as valued experts.

We highly recommend hiring an expert to help you and your team develop your brand guidelines. Unless you were a brand strategist and designer in your last career, you don't have the skills to do this at a professional level. There's a lot that goes into brand guidelines, including visual design elements, key language, and rules about how and when to use those things. Professional consultants will help you get this right so your brand both stands out from the competition and accurately reflects the culture of your team.

Ideally, you'll end up with libraries of imagery and language for everything: sellers, buyers, staging, promotional pieces, charitable causes, and more. Your team will be able to pull from the library as needed, and you won't have to worry about the brand getting diluted from each person interpreting it in their own way. That's how you keep your brand unified over time.

That said, branding isn't a one-and-done process. You'll probably have to add to your libraries over time as different needs come up, and you may want to refresh the look and feel after a few years. However, if you do this right the first time, a refresh is easy because it's just a superficial polish—the underlying culture and brand are still the same.

Defining your culture and brand is a big project the first time you do it. If you do it well, though, you won't have to do a major overhaul for many years. Of course, things can and should shift slightly over time. As we mentioned earlier, it's good to step back with your team at least once a year and ask whether the values, principles, and branding language still feel like a good fit.

But we're talking about your fundamental identity: who you are and how you do business. It makes sense that you shouldn't need to change it much from year to year. If you do, that's a sign that you never settled on a clear identity in the first place, and it might be wise to invest in a top-notch branding consultant.

Next up, we'll talk about another defining aspect of your team: its structure.

Chapter 5

TEAM STRUCTURE

We've already pointed out that most real estate teams aren't really teams at all. So it may not surprise you to learn that when it comes to team structure, there usually isn't one!

But don't take our word for it. Ask any team leader what *type* of team they have. They won't know; they probably won't even understand what you mean.

That's because most team leaders never consider structure. They simply hire organically, with no long-term vision as to who would play which roles or why. As soon as an agent makes the decision to form a team, they start adding bodies—acquaintances who work under the same brokerage, local agents with a solid reputation, family members looking for a career change, you name it. And as long as there's business, they add more.

Leaders who form teams this way are simply reacting to opportunities and operational constraints. There is no planning or goal setting, no consideration of complementary strengths, and no conceptualization of the many roles necessary to make a small business function.

We've seen far too many agents form teams of three to five people, all of whom have about the same amount of experience selling similar listings in the same market. Can you picture a doctor, just to take one example, hiring four other doctors—no receptionist, no nurse, no business manager—and expecting business to take off?

Of course not. But in real estate, a star agent who's looking for more business goes for coffee with a friend . . . and leaves Starbucks with a new business partner. Or they can't stand saying no to an opportunity, so they go hire a buyer's agent as soon as they have more business than they can handle.

There are no job descriptions, no formal agreements, no clear vision for how they'll work together. Inevitably, this leads to poor productivity, messy conflicts, and even legal battles.

This kind of transaction-driven team growth exposes a team leader to all manner of problems. You'll find yourself stuck managing underperformers. If leads are shared equally among agents regardless of track record, your stronger agents may come to believe they're not being properly valued. Key roles may go unfilled, and inexperienced agents may fail to get the reps required to develop their skills. These are the failures that cause team leaders to throw up their hands and say, correctly, that they were doing better on their own.

The bottom line is that structure should be dictated by a vision of how you want your team to function, not by the immediate pressure of transaction volume.

The team structure can be anything you want it to be, and it can change over time, but you need to start with a plan. You need to understand how your decisions affect the way you and the team will function. The goal is to create an environment of productivity for everyone. In this regard, as in so many others, a real estate team is no different than any business in any industry.

In this chapter, we explore the three primary structure options, as well as a few other factors to consider. We'll walk through the most important decisions, so you can figure out which option fits best with your vision and preferences.

True Teams

We'll start with the most powerful type of team, what we like to call a true team. On a true team, agents collaborate closely to maximize overall team production. There's no individual victory; you win or lose as a group.

Think team sports, like football. Every role is specialized and well-defined, on the field and off. Even if there is a star player, that person can't win by themselves. They have to depend on and work with everyone else. Most importantly, the star player isn't the team leader. The leader is the coach—the strategic thinker who trains, directs, and supports the players.

This is the most powerful type of team for two reasons.

One is that it allows for specialization, which dramatically raises the potential for synergy. For example, Dana's agents handle the buy side *or* the sell side, but not both. On your team, you could have specialized agents for different price points, geographic areas, or property types (like residential versus commercial, or single family versus condominium). Dana's office staff is also highly specialized. In addition to her executive assistant, she has experts in operations, marketing, staging, and inspections. There's even a listing liaison available during busy times to oversee the logistics of each transaction.

When each person focuses on one area, they master it faster because they get more reps in less time. Instead of being passably competent at many things, each team member is great at one thing and relies on their teammates for everything else. Collaboration is mandatory, and competition is moot, since there's little overlap between roles. As a result, everything gets done faster and better.

That's the whole point of a team: the whole is greater than the sum of its parts. It's a major attraction for both your team members and your clients. The team members get to focus on their strengths and develop their skills quickly, and the clients get better results and a smoother experience—not to mention peace of mind, knowing that there's a whole team supporting them instead of just one person.

Specialization does bring some challenges. As team leader, you'll need to set up crystal clear protocols to handle all the situations that might generate conflict. For example, what happens when a buyer's agent gets a listing lead through their personal network, or vice versa? You need to define and communicate your team's process for such eventualities.

On Dana's team, the agent who comes across the lead that's not in their area *must* offer it to the appropriate specialist. But if the lead is declined, the agent who brought it in is free to do the deal themselves. Tellingly, Dana has found that in most cases, her agents don't want to "switch sides" because it takes more effort, and they know their colleagues can do a better job. They'd rather let the specialist handle it knowing the reverse scenario will also happen for them.

The second reason a true team is the most powerful model is that it maximizes your ability to extract yourself from the business, temporarily (like when you go on vacation) or permanently (when you retire and sell the business). As team leader, you're the coach, not the star player. Your agents need you for strategic guidance, accountability, and training, but you're not actually doing deals, which means you have a lot more control over your time and physical location.

It takes time to achieve this. As a solo agent, you bring in all the leads and execute all the transactions. As you build your team, you'll delegate more and more of the execution, until you're just bringing in leads and distributing them to your agents. Then you'll start to shift the lead generation responsibilities to the agents, so they don't depend solely on you.

Even when you're not generating all the leads, you're still providing massive value to your team members. Because they're specialized and interdependent, they can't do this work alone—at least, not at the level of performance they can achieve within the team. Even in their own prospecting, they rely on the team's brand and reputation. They also depend on you to analyze the market, craft the team's client-facing messaging, provide training and feedback, intervene in tough cases, and keep the business healthy.

However, none of that requires you to be present constantly, which means you have much more flexibility to take time away from the office than a solo agent does. Your role also no longer revolves around your personal identity. Someone else can learn how to do all the things we just mentioned, which means someone else can one day buy the business, and it will continue to function well.

The major drawback of a true team is that most agents know how to be star players, but they don't know how to be coaches. This change in role is dramatic, and many agents fail to make it. Either they don't coach at all, leaving the team effectively leaderless, or they try to do both and become completely overwhelmed.

If you're going to build a true team, you *have* to let go of being the rainmaker. Your individual production is no longer important. In fact, the goal is for you to have *zero* production. That's what maximizes both your freedom and the value of your business.

In terms of size, true teams work best with eight to twelve people. Go too far beyond that, and they will fall apart; large groups simply can't collaborate closely enough to make this highly interdependent model work. Once you get above about fifteen people, the mini brokerage model is your only option.

Mini Brokerages

A mini brokerage is exactly what it sounds like. Unlike a true team, it's not all for one and one for all. Each person's goal is to maximize their own production, and the goal of the business is to create systems that enhance individual performance. In this model, your job as team leader is to build those systems and make sure they provide enough value to justify the splits you take on your agents' transactions.

This is where big brokerages fail. They struggle to provide tangible value, especially to top agents, who play brokerages off each other to drive up their splits. The brokerages, desperate to keep those big-name players, often agree to pay them 90 percent or even more. That cuts deep into the brokerage's bottom line and makes it even harder to provide value to its agents.

To make this model work, you have to strike the right balance. Your systems have to make agents more successful than they would be on their own, and the splits you charge have to cover the cost of building and maintaining those systems—with profit leftover. Otherwise, you're better off on your own.

What exactly do we mean by systems? In short, everything that helps agents do their jobs. That's not limited to services like marketing, listing management, and transaction coordination. It also includes training, support, advice, brand recognition, and even community. Big brokerages claim to provide some of these things, but they're not tailored to the agent, and the lines to the advantages are long.

This is where so many team leaders fall short. They bring people under their umbrella but don't actually do much to maximize their production. Those people end up contributing little to nothing to the business's bottom line—sometimes they even *cost* money. That's a complete waste of your time and energy, which is why it's so crucial to actively engage in elevating the performance of your agents.

In a mini brokerage, unlike a true team, agents are typically generalists, not specialists. Any agent can represent anyone—buyer, seller, any price point, any geography. The big advantage here is that the team isn't getting in the way of agents doing business.

On the other hand, teams of generalists inevitably see lots of competition and conflict among agents. And it's more challenging for the team leader to decide how to distribute leads because in theory, anyone can take anything, but in reality, some people are a better fit for a given lead than others, in terms of expertise and personality. A truly "fair" system will lead to less-than-ideal matches, while a better matchmaking system will generate bad blood and accusations of favoritism.

For this reason, agents tend to bring in more of their own leads and depend less on leads provided by the team lead. This makes it easy to weed out agents who can't sell on their own. Underperformers probably won't join you in the first place if you're not lobbing them easy leads, so mini brokerages often attract excellent producers. Also, this makes it easier to get your life back. As with a true team, the less responsibility you have for generating leads, the more freedom you have with your time.

But this independence has downsides as well. For one, it leads to higher turnover as agents develop their own networks and move up and out. And since you're not always providing leads, you have less leverage over your agents' behavior. That makes it harder to get agents to conform to the team culture and ways of working. Perhaps the biggest drawback of the Mini Brokerage model is the cost. It is a high-overhead model with many fixed costs that are not easy to unwind quickly. Running this kind of team requires capital and tremendous financial discipline. You have to know your margins and numbers inside and out.

Again, the key with this model is to find ways to provide real value to agents—support and resources that meaningfully increase their productivity. When agents feel the benefits of doing things your way, resistance decreases dramatically. If it doesn't, the agent in question simply isn't a good fit for your team and, in the end, probably isn't going to be very profitable for you.

Rainmaker Teams

If you want a small team where you can keep your role as the star player, a rainmaker team is what you need. In this model, you are responsible for the majority of the production, and the team's goal is to maximize your capabilities. Unlike true teams and mini brokerages, it's not wildly different from what you already do as a solo agent. That's why this model is a good option for agents who love the top-seller role and don't see themselves giving that up.

It's similar to what professional athletes do in solo sports, like tennis. The player has a support team whose job is to help them achieve their highest potential, which might include a coach, a trainer, a manager, a practice partner, and so on. Those people all play vital roles, but they don't go out on the court and win matches.

Same on a rainmaker team. It usually starts when a highly productive agent hires an assistant, who takes on organizational and administrative tasks so the agent has more time to sell. It might grow to include multiple assistants, an office manager, and other agents who can take on excess business the rainmaker can't handle. However, those agents don't focus on going out and getting their own business; they just take the leads the rainmaker gives them.

To make this work at a large scale and still have a life, you need serious administrative support. Not an entry-level assistant who can handle only the basics. We're talking about a chief of staff, a marketing director, an operations manager—experienced people who can be entrusted with core aspects of the business. Delegating those responsibilities is the only way to free up your time so you can focus on lead generation.

If you don't hire the right support staff, things will get messy. We've seen this firsthand: rainmakers who know their teams have major problems in core business areas, like operations and HR, but never solve those problems because they don't have the time or expertise. So the problems fester, sapping productivity and wasting resources year after year. The only thing anybody can do is push harder, and that is *not* what we're aiming for here.

When rainmaker teams are run right, there are some distinct advantages. One, as we've already mentioned, is that they make the best use of your current skills. You're already a rainmaker by yourself, and with this type of team, you have the bandwidth to make even more rain. Your role doesn't change drastically, so the transition will be easier.

Another plus is that these teams tend to have lower agent turnover. There's nothing agents like better than leads served up on a platter; as long as you deliver, they will stick around. Plus, you can collect bigger splits because you're bringing clients to the table.

But the rainmaker team has potential pitfalls too. Part of your job will be transitioning clients to other team members, and this can be tricky. After all, you have earned a strong reputation in your market as an individual. Many clients will balk at being handed off; they reached out to *you*, after all, not to a person they may perceive as a junior staffer. You have to be able to sell your team, not just yourself, as you learned in Chapter 4.

You'll also have to invest time and money in training your team to do business your way. Otherwise, you won't be able to trust them to take care of the clients you give them. To protect and build the whole team's reputation, everyone needs to run these relationships right. And when things aren't working out, you have to be ready to fire quickly, before the fallout damages the rest of the team and your brand.

And of course, as we've mentioned many times, the more your business depends on you, the less value it has to anyone else. If you are personally responsible for bringing in all the clients, how will the business perform when someone else takes your place? There's really no telling, which makes it harder to sell.

Problems also arise when the market slows down. In those times, rainmakers want to hold onto their leads, which leaves less overflow for the other agents on their team. That's a surefire way to create tension and sow distrust within your team. They are dependent on you; they don't have the skills to win their own business. For that reason, it's crucial to have a crystal clear policy on how leads will be distributed, so team members understand what to expect.

In general, about five people is a comfortable size for a rainmaker team. The model doesn't work well for more than ten or so. At that point, you would need to think about becoming either a true team or a mini brokerage.

Ownership

Regardless of which type of team you decide to build, there's always the question of ownership. Are you the sole owner, or are there others involved? The answer has important implications, and ideally, you should consider them carefully before making a decision.

Here are the major types of ownership structure:

- Sole proprietorship: one agent owns the team
- Dual partnership: a fifty-fifty split; this is the most common type of partnership we see
- Group partnership: four, five, or more agents band together to share services
- Family ownership: partners are family members, which can create special challenges
- Silent financial partner: an investor who is not involved in running the business; this is uncommon in real estate

In any of these structures, critical details are up to you, including how much each person owns, what their roles and responsibilities are, and how much influence they have over major decisions.

Shared ownership has its advantages. For one, the financial burden is shared. For most real estate teams, startup costs are not exorbitant. But that doesn't mean they're nonexistent, and dividing them can help ease the transition from solo agent to team leader. Liability, too, is shared.

However, shared ownership comes with potential drawbacks. As we've seen time and time again, you can't really know your partner until the team is in operation. You may *think* you know them. You may have been colleagues or friends for years, or perhaps they're even family. But people behave in unpredictable ways when they have skin in the game and there's money to be allocated.

If there's an even number of partners and you have a major disagreement, the friction can be extreme because there's nobody to break a tie. Such disagreements are often caused by poor planning or the lack of a shared vision for the business. Partners need to start out closely aligned and remain that way even through hardship.

For a partnership to be successful, you have to treat it as nothing less than a marriage. The partnership, not your individual needs and beliefs, must come first. Everybody must be willing to compromise, to take one for the team. This can be a challenge in the me-first real estate world, where top agents succeed by doing things their own way.

The partnerships that work best are equal—fifty-fifty. Sure, the business is coming from *someone*, and in the back of your mind, you surely know who. Some partners are more "equal" than others. But the moment you start keeping score, wondering if you're getting your fair share, you introduce tension that helps no one and only undermines the partnership.

Compensation

How should you compensate your team members? This is a simple question with many possible answers. Which one is right for you depends in large part on your team structure, which is why we're bringing it up now. Like structure, compensation is something that most team leaders don't think about strategically, and that leads to all kinds of problems down the road.

When designing your compensation structure, there are three questions to consider:

1. Does it support the business model?
2. Is it competitive in the marketplace?
3. Is it fair?

Let's tackle the first one: Does your compensation structure support your business model?

This is the most important question because if the answer is no, none of the other questions matter. You need to make a profit on each team member—there's no point in hiring people just to grow the gross. If your compensation model isn't profitable for you, you may as well not have a team.

In general, most team leaders are too generous. They don't think about compensation systematically, and they don't know how much they can really afford to pay. So they're at the mercy of their team members' demands. Agents come to them asking for higher splits, and more often than not, the team leader gives in because they don't want to lose the agent.

In fact, it's not uncommon for team leaders to go so far as to match what the brokerage split would be if the agent weren't on the team. That leaves them with only the difference between the splits—maybe 10 or 20 percent of the gross commission, or less.

That is *not enough* to sustain your business. Every team member costs you money, typically around $40K to $50K per year. They cost you time and effort, too, probably more than you bargained for and almost certainly more than you realize. Your time is worth a lot—you could be out there selling instead of supporting your team members. Most team leaders never account for that opportunity cost.

Plus, you're the one taking on the risk of the fixed costs that go with running a business. You have rent, insurance, and salaried team members to worry about. You have to keep enough savings in the bank to absorb a bad year (for Dana, that's more than $1 million). Remember, you could be making a 25 percent referral fee for no risk, effort, or time at all. So your team members better be worth your while financially.

Most team leaders have no clue how much profit they're making on each agent, but this is a crucial number to track. At a minimum—a *bare minimum*—you should be making at least $100K from each team member before expenses. With the average cost per agent at $40K to $50K per year, that's about $50K of profit, which barely justifies the time and hassle. If you're paying agents more than 50 percent of your net commission (after your split with the brokerage), you're probably paying more than you can afford.

There's a nonfinancial aspect to this first question as well: Does your compensation structure encourage the *behaviors* that support your business model? In other words, do your team members get financially rewarded for doing the things that help the team succeed?

For example, Dana has a true team, so collaboration is a crucial behavior she wants to encourage. So, she pays a "team fee" to each team member whenever a transaction closes. To qualify for the fee, the team member has to be in the on-call rotation for weekends, and they have to take on a responsibility that contributes to the team as a whole. She finds that without the team fee, people are less quick to step up when their teammates need support.

What kind of behavior do you need from your team, and how can you tie compensation to that? You might choose to pay bonuses based on production or other measures of job performance. You could offer a raise in split contingent on meeting certain targets. There are many, many different ways to use money to encourage (or discourage) specific behaviors.

Now, the second question: Is your compensation competitive in the marketplace?

The answer depends on what value your team members get from you. What services and support do you provide? Where do the leads come from? Who covers costs? The more value you provide, the lower your compensation can be. A low split can still be an attractive proposition to an agent if everything else you offer is going to make them happier and more productive.

Unfortunately, agents tend to overvalue their contribution to the team and undervalue what they receive from it. It's up to you to make sure they're aware of everything you do for them, including the risks you take on their behalf. You need to be clear on this for yourself as well, or you'll find it hard to resist when your agents insist they deserve a higher split.

When that happens, remind them that this is a performance-based industry. Agents can make lots of money if they produce, but there are no handouts. The best way to make more is to sell more—a bump in their split is nothing compared to the money they can make from increasing their volume.

Finally, the third question: Is your compensation structure fair?

In this case, "fair" means a few different things. First of all, it means consistent. People who are doing the same work at the same level should be compensated the same. There should be logic behind the compensation decisions you make—like what the base rate is, when someone gets a raise, or how much their bonus is—and that logic should apply equally to everyone.

Compensation may be confidential, but you should act as if it were not. What if everyone on your team found out what everyone else was making? Would they be outraged by seemingly arbitrary differences, or would there be clear and objective reasons to justify the numbers?

Create a system, and stay within it. Inconsistency is bad for team morale and bad for your finances.

"Fair" also means there should be a clear link between the person's work and any variable compensation you might offer. Be very careful about tying pay to outcomes the person has no control over.

For example, team leaders often like to pay their assistants a percentage of the commission instead of a salary. That saves them from the risk of having a fixed cost to cover when business is slow. But is it fair?

That depends on how much influence the assistant has on how many and how fast deals get done. If the answer is very little, a salary would be more appropriate. You can add some commission-based compensation on top of that to give them skin in the game, which incentivizes them to move transactions along quicker. But the less influence they have over production, the more their compensation should be weighted toward salary.

"Fair" means transparent too. There should be no mystery here. Everyone needs to know in advance how much, when, and how they'll be paid. They need to understand all the factors that might affect their pay, including their bonuses, benefits, and potential future raises. Everything should be in writing, and if it's going to change, you need to provide notice well in advance.

As you can see, there is no one answer to the compensation question. It's a complex issue, and to make the right choices, you need to understand your whole business, especially your team structure. In the end, it's about providing value for value. The value you provide includes not only monetary compensation, but also all the services, resources, and support you give your team members. In exchange, each person needs to make a significant contribution to your bottom line—not just the top line.

A Note on Legalities

One of the most confusing and potentially fraught issues you'll face when forming a team is deciding whether members will be employees or independent contractors. This issue is complex; it's easy to run afoul of laws and regulations if you're not careful.

In general, employee status will give you greater control over when, where, and how team members work. This comes at the cost of payroll taxes and benefits, but it's often worth it. However, the industry has lobbied hard to make it almost impossible for agents to be classified as employees.

All we can say is this: do your homework. Work with an HR attorney or consultant who is intimately familiar with your state's labor laws, so you can make an educated decision that works for your team and your state.

The team structure you choose becomes the heart of your business model, and lack of clarity on your model is a recipe for trouble—financial trouble, operational trouble, and people trouble. That's why structure is one of the first things we ask about when team leaders come to us for help. More often than not, they've never thought about team structure from a strategic perspective, if at all.

Well, now you have. You've seen that there are three fundamental types of teams, each with different purposes and internal dynamics. If you want maximum synergy and are willing to transform from the star player into the head coach, build a true team. If you want a very large team or prefer a less interdependent approach, build a mini brokerage. If you want to continue as the star player but leverage yourself to the max, build a rainmaker team.

Within these models, there is plenty of room for variety, but you need to choose one and understand what it takes to make it work. Ultimately, it's a lack of this understanding that drives most of the team problems we see. True teams with no head coach, mini brokerages with no productivity systems, rainmaker teams with inadequate support—these things happen all the time. You can avoid them by choosing your structure intentionally and respecting its requirements and limitations.

In the next chapter, we'll tackle the final major decision to make as you set up your team: your business strategy.

Chapter 6

DEFINING YOUR STRATEGY

Over the last ten years, Dana's business has tripled three times. She started with just one assistant and $50 million in gross sales. Today, she has reached almost $400 million and leads a team of six agents and six support staff.

This kind of growth is rare. Most teams, like most solo agents, struggle to grow consistently without burning out.

So what's the difference? What is the key to Dana's team's success?

Some might think it's charisma—which Dana has in spades—but it's not. To be sure, she's charming and personable, but many agents can say the same. Typically, top agents who enjoy enough success to even consider forming a team have attractive personalities. In this industry, that's nothing special.

So is it sheer hard work? Nope. In fact, unlike most team leaders, Dana doesn't let work take over her entire life. She takes set days off each week and goes on vacation multiple times a year.

Plus, her daily work routine is highly structured, which keeps it from getting out of control.

Instead of working harder, Dana works *smarter*—and that's the secret to her success.

We know, it sounds cliché. But "working smarter" is not just an empty phrase—it's a powerful shift in perspective and behavior. It means having a clear strategy: a set of boundaries around where, how, and with whom you are going to do business.

Most agents don't have this. They simply chase whatever leads cross their path, with no idea what their competitive advantage is or how to leverage it. Their only "plan" for getting more business is to work more, but that's not sustainable or scalable.

Chasing deals is part of the "me" mentality. Once you're a team leader, you need a "we" mentality, which means focusing your activity where you have a competitive advantage. In this chapter, you'll learn how to uncover that advantage and design your business model around it.

This is just the first of three phases in the life cycle of your business. Phase 1 is about preparing to grow. It's no use piling more people into a boat that leaks, which is exactly how most real estate teams are built—and why they sink. First, you need to fix those holes and set the right course. Otherwise, your growth will be a mess that gets harder and harder to bail yourself out of.

Once that's done, you can think about Phases 2 and 3, where you'll apply and scale your business model. We'll touch on those later, but first, let's focus on the key question: What's your competitive advantage?

Get Your Data Together

Most teams don't have a strategy because they operate based on feelings and instinct, not data. Ask them to show you all the business they've ever done and they'll give you (if anything) five different files in five different formats, with key transaction data missing and errors all over the place. This is what happens when everyone spends all their time chasing the next deal—no one is tracking or analyzing what has already happened.

All this inconsistent and confusing data is impossible to sort, segment, and analyze. So it's impossible to tell what's working in the business and what isn't. Instead of learning from the past, the team just plows forward. They develop no understanding of where to spend their time and resources, or whom to avoid. Every lead looks equally attractive.

That's a fantasy. Every lead is *not* created equal. Some have a high probability of resulting in a successful deal, while others are virtually guaranteed to lead nowhere and waste a whole lot of time along the way. Without data, you can't tell the difference.

You also can't back up your marketing claims. Top-performing team? Number one in your area? Below-average time on the market? Above-average sale price? No one is buying it if you don't have the evidence to show for it. Feelings are not facts, and today's consumers know the difference.

Without data-based insight into your business, you only have personality to fall back on. At first, that seems like an effective tool for winning people over. But in the long run, it's a weak foundation for a business. Personality only works when you're there in the room with prospects and clients. The bigger your team gets, the less often that will be the case, and sadly, you can't transfer your magical personality to your team members.

So, if you want your sales to be based on something stronger, you need data. The first step is simple: collect every transaction you've ever touched, and put them all in one database.

This is a one-time project. It will probably be painful, but it's well worth the time you'll invest. Record every transaction in detail, and in a standard way that allows for easy analysis. Include all significant metrics: characteristics of the property, neighborhood, asking price, sales price, days on market, and so on.

This can be a simple spreadsheet, or you can use a program specifically designed for real estate. Keep in mind that whatever you choose, your entire team will be using it for years to come. This is a *commitment*—from now on, every detail of every transaction goes in your database as soon as possible. So go with whatever technology will make it easiest for everyone to use the database and keep it up to date.

Analyze Your Business

Once your transaction database is built, it's time to put it to use. First, you'll want to study where your business is coming from. Break it down by geographic area, property type, and price point. Look at who your clients are (age, occupation, family size, etc.) and how they found out about you (if you haven't been asking that question, start now).

We bet you'll find that 50 percent or more of your business comes from one sweet spot—a particular combination of geography, property type, price point, and client type. The rest is all over the map, literally and figuratively. And guess what? You're probably spending far more of your time, effort, and money chasing business *outside* your sweet spot than in it.

We see this all the time with individual agents and teams alike. It's a fundamental misalignment between what you're investing in and what's actually working for you. Instead of playing to your strengths, you focus on your weak areas, where you don't have a competitive advantage.

In real estate, it's always smarter to double down where you're already strong. Here's why: even the top producers in any given market rarely have more than 10 percent market share. That means they're still not getting 90 percent of the business, even where they're most dominant. There is plenty of room to grow, and they're much more likely to grow quickly where they are already the top contender instead of the underdog.

For example, Dana's team is the top player in Lafayette, California, real estate. They do three times more business there than anyone else, and because of that, she has a massive competitive advantage. People recognize her brand, her team has many connections, and they know more about the local neighborhoods and market dynamics than anyone.

And yet, as dominant as Dana's team is, their market share hovers just over 10 percent. This still leaves enormous room for growth. In fact, about half the transactions in Lafayette are handled by agents who do only *one* transaction there a year. Those are ripe opportunities. There's no reason to go into another market where her brand carries less weight, people don't know her team, and she doesn't know the landscape.

Here's the kicker: the more Dana's team builds their advantage in Lafayette, the harder it is for upstart competitors to gain a foothold. Granted, there's still plenty of competition—again, over 80 percent of the market isn't theirs. But for a new agent, entering a market so dominated by one team is not exactly an attractive proposition. By focusing on their strengths, Dana's team gets stronger and stronger, and their competitive advantage gets easier to maintain.

On the flip side, consider another big team we know (in a different location) that does the opposite. Instead of focusing on one sweet spot, each agent is allowed to do business wherever they want, with whomever they want. This team has three times more agents than Dana's, but they do only twice as much business, and their maximum market share in any given area is only 3 percent.

That means they're not getting in the reps required to develop the depth of brand recognition and market insight that Dana's team has. If they had 10 percent market share in just one area, how much more business could they do?

Bottom line: you can't be everything to everyone. It's tempting to try, but that means going a mile wide and an inch deep—you spread yourself too thin and never build any real expertise. It's the inch-wide, mile-deep approach that makes you knowledgeable, trustworthy, and desirable. Better to be the go-to agent for a specific type of deal than a generalist who doesn't stand out in anything.

So use your newly gathered and sorted data to choose the niche in which you'll be most successful, where you have the most experience and the most connections already. Remember, geography is only one aspect of your sweet spot; don't forget to consider price point, property type, and client type as well. In the long run, the goal is to do 100 percent of your business in your sweet spot.

If you're just starting out, you may not have the data yet to know what your sweet spot is. In that case, we have two pieces of advice. First, track everything religiously and watch how things are evolving. It won't take long to start seeing trends. Second, seek out areas in which no single agent or team has more than 10 percent market share. A market like that is wide open, so you shouldn't have too much trouble getting established there.

Maximize the Client Experience

In addition to choosing your future strategic direction, you also need to protect your existing client base. After all, no matter how clear your strategy is, you can't get far without plenty of repeat and referral clients. Ask any top-producing agent or team what their repeat and referral rate is, and you'll hear numbers like 50, 60, even 80 or 90 percent.

Why is this so crucial? Because repeat and referral clients are better in every way. It takes less time and money to get them, and they're more likely to trust you, which means it's easier to get to a good outcome for all. And the virtuous cycle continues, because once they've had a good experience with you, they'll tell their friends and come back to you for their future real estate needs. More begets more, in the most natural and effortless way.

Well, not totally effortless. For this to work, your clients have to have a great experience—no dropped balls or screwups that damage the relationship and undermine their trust in you. Of course, there will always be tough choices and unexpected hiccups in any real estate deal. However, it's your team's job to prepare the client for those things and guide them through the process as seamlessly as possible.

You may think you already do a pretty good job of this. After all, it seems like most of the time, you close the deal on good terms with your clients. They seem happy with the outcome. They say they'll come back and recommend you to their friends.

Everyone says that, but on average, less than 20 percent actually do it. If you don't already have a repeat and referral rate above 50 percent—and ideally it should be closer to 100 percent—you have work to do.

Most agents don't take this seriously enough. If they close a deal, they think they've won. Maybe that person will come back in the future, maybe not—that's years down the line anyway. What's the big deal?

They're not thinking about the lifetime value of the client. If you do only one deal, that client was worth one commission. But if you give them such a great experience that you become their go-to real estate team, the one they swear by and always recommend, that one client could lead to three, ten, even fifty or more deals over the years.

To make that happen, you have to plug the holes in the boat. That means building systems and training personnel to provide clients the best possible experience—all the things you'll learn in the next section of this book.

The benefits of hole-plugging extend to your team members too. When things don't go smoothly, they also get frustrated. No one wants to be the one telling the client that a mistake was made or something went wrong. No one wants to work in a team where people aren't clear on what to do or how to do it, and therefore fail to deliver for their teammates. That leads to high turnover, which is expensive, time consuming, and emotionally draining.

Plugging holes makes everyone happier and will help prevent future leaks—from your client base and your team. We'll get to all that in Chapters 7 through 10.

Beyond Phase 1: Applying and Scaling Your Model

Once you've defined your model and gotten your house in order, you'll be ready for serious growth. This happens in two distinct phases.

In Phase 2, you focus on applying and refining your model in the markets you presently serve. This is where you double down on your sweet spot and focus your marketing efforts and energy there.

You also work on maximizing the lifetime value of your current clients. Each one should be the source of multiple transactions, through repeat business and referrals. Yes, we said *each one*! Your system needs to be client oriented, not transaction oriented; you should view every client as a source of at least three future sales. These relationships compound over time to provide an ever-expanding source of future business.

Too many agents are passive about referrals and reviews, thinking of them as something that either happens or doesn't. We're going to help you change that by building a team that's so strong, referrals will be expected.

The challenging thing about Phase 2 is that this is where you'll begin turning down certain opportunities. This is completely foreign to agents who've spent a career chasing every lead, regardless of geography, price point, or other factors. But remember, you cannot max out the potential of your sweet spot if you're spending time and energy elsewhere. Leads and marketing opportunities will cross your path all the time—but not all of them are worth your time. If you can't learn to prioritize and say no sometimes, you won't find the sustainable growth you want.

Only when you've perfected your model and dominated your sweet spot should you think of moving on to Phase 3. This is where you scale your model, bringing it to new neighborhoods and markets.

We advise patience here. Don't rush to Phase 3; it doesn't make sense to scale a model you haven't mastered yet. By the time you've truly mastered your model and thoroughly tested it in Phase 2, you will have built relationships and brand equity that will allow you to remain dominant in your original sweet spot while transferring some of your focus to a new area.

Sustainable growth is not about chasing deals. That's the "me" strategy, and while it may have won you enough business to max out your individual capacity, it's not an effective way to scale a team. In terms of strategy, going from "me" to "we" requires you to identify and pursue a clear business model. This is a difficult evolution for most agents because it means drawing boundaries—defining business you will and will not do.

But nothing worthwhile is easy. The "me" to "we" transition is essential, because if you try to be everything to everybody, you'll end up being nothing to anyone.

PART III

REGULAR SEASON EXECUTION

These are the key elements that make it possible to handle high volumes of business and still deliver an outstanding client experience. They include your systems, your people, your marketing, and your ability to continuously improve.

Chapter 7

SYSTEMS AND PROCESSES

Imagine this scenario.

You land a new listing. The relationship starts off in great form, with optimistic predictions of a quick sale at a high price.

But three weeks after you post the listing, there has been almost no activity. You know from experience that this means you need to reduce the price. But before doing so, you're looking at a hard conversation with the seller, who didn't see this coming and is understandably disappointed.

This common scenario does not make for a great client experience. Naturally, it's unlikely to lead to repeat and referral business.

Now picture this instead.

In your listing presentation, you explain to the seller that based on data and your experience, you know that the first eighteen days of a listing are crucial. You can list at their ideal price, and things may work out. However, you explain, if there's no significant activity during those crucial eighteen days, they'll need to consider a 5 to 10 percent price reduction.

You keep the seller informed of all activity, so by the time day eighteen rolls around, they can see that their ideal price is too high, even before you initiate the price reduction conversation. They're disappointed, but *not in you*. You warned them this might happen, and they saw it coming. They were emotionally prepared.

That's a much better client experience, and it's all thanks to your *process*.

A process is simply a series of steps for anything in your business that will be repeated. A system is a set of processes. Your business should have processes and systems for absolutely *everything*.

Systems are the lynchpin for creating two essential results in your business: (1) a great client experience and (2) quality of life for you and your team.

You can see both outcomes in this imaginary (but all too real) scenario. Systems create trust, consistency, and clarity for the client, so they can feel confident that everything is happening the right way. Because of that, those tough conversations get way easier, so you and your team can stress less. Plus, that great client experience leads to repeat and referral business, which is less time consuming and more profitable for your team. Everybody wins.

In the last chapter, you learned about working smarter through strategy. Now, you're going to take it even further with systems. Most real estate agents have no systems. If they do have processes, they don't use them consistently. Instead, they keep all the steps in their heads and hope they don't miss anything.

That's hard enough for a solo agent, especially as you get busier. On a team, it's complete chaos. In this chapter, you'll learn why systems are so essential, which ones you need in your business, and how to build them.

You Can't Scale Chaos

Real estate is a highly emotional business. After all, you're dealing with not only your clients' biggest asset but also with the foundation of their day-to-day life—the place they live. It's natural and inevitable that they're all wrapped up in their hopes and desires, most of which are unrealistic.

Your job is to be rational, calm, and tactical, so you can see the forest for the trees. But if you have no systems, it only adds to the emotional turmoil for both you and the client. As you saw in the imaginary scenario above, the lack of a process created unnecessary stress for the seller, which in turn created stress for the agent. It's a messy, ugly feedback loop.

With systems, on the other hand, you can look ahead, explain the landscape to the client, anticipate various outcomes, and see around corners. You can be proactive and strategic, which helps you stay calm and reassures your client. Most importantly, you can create good outcomes *consistently*.

Steve compares home-selling to what happens when the kicker comes on the field in a football game. These are some of the most emotionally intense moments of any game. The kicker's only job is to kick the ball between the uprights. This may seem like a simple thing to do, but a field goal or extra point often decides the game, so it's a crucial task. Plus, the kicker only has 1.3 seconds to do it before the opposing team is on top of the ball. The slightest deviation from perfection could screw up the kick and cost the team the game.

And it's not up to the kicker alone either. He needs the rest of the team to snap the ball perfectly, hold it perfectly, and successfully block all the defensive players from reaching the ball. The whole team has to work in concert. There's a *lot* of pressure and many ways to fail.

As we write, the best kicker in the NFL, Justin Tucker, has kicked sixty-one consecutive successful field goals in the fourth quarter and overtime—the most high stakes moments of the game.

How does he do it? As he put it, he focuses on perfecting the *system*. Snap, hold, kick. It's the same process every time. His feelings don't matter. The emotionally charged circumstances are irrelevant. When the team gets the nuts and bolts right, the ball takes care of itself.

The same is true for your business. Systems take the emotion out of it, so your team doesn't fumble just because a client is upset, or an agent is tired, or your office manager is distracted. They keep everyone on the same page about what to do and how. They also ensure that you and your team are accountable to each other and to the client.

That's why Dana says, "Don't blame the person; blame the process." When something goes wrong, the process is the first place she looks for flaws. If you're depending on people to remember tasks and interpret guidelines their own way, *of course* mistakes will be made. A great process makes it impossible for anyone to say, "I didn't know," "I forgot," or "I thought you meant this, not that."

Most agents never perfect these nuts and bolts. Each time they go on a listing presentation, it's as if they've never done it before—even if they have years of experience. They spend hours pulling together materials when most of it should be done already; they should be able to just grab the book, stick in the comparative market analysis, and go. Snap. Hold. Kick.

Nothing in your business should ever be a mad dash. Everything should be scripted and practiced. But as we've said before, agents get used to the mad dash, and it becomes the norm. That's when mistakes happen—like you arrive at the client's house and realize you have the CMA for the wrong listing. Then you have to tap dance to cover up your mistake and cross your fingers that the client doesn't notice.

You simply can't be great at what you do if you're scrambling at the last minute. It's exhausting, and it's not scalable. Even if you pull it off as a solo agent, you'll never have a high-performing team without repeatable, reliable systems.

Dana remembers the mad dash well, and she hated the anxiety and uncertainty of it. She wanted to know in advance exactly what she was doing, so she could focus on nailing it. When she sat down for a presentation, she wanted all her attention on the clients and their home. That's why she began building systems. And the more time she spent putting in those systems and processes, the less stress she faced.

Time and time again, Dana's team hears from sellers that their presentations are hands down the best. This isn't luck or coincidence. It's because the team has a system.

Why don't more agents, and even teams, follow suit?

They're stuck in the chase-convince-close paradigm, so focused on the next deal that they never take the time to build processes and systems. Without systems, they always have to scramble and improvise. Work inefficiency is a hard habit to break. The "blender effect" is real. It's that feeling you have at the end of a full day. You were busy all day . . . you just don't know what you actually got done that truly matters. So it feels like there's no time for anything but the chase.

Once you fall into this trap, it's tough to escape. You don't have the time to do the things that will ultimately save you time.

The result: everything feels out of control, all the time. And that's the worst feeling in the world when you're dealing with someone's biggest asset. At any given moment, you have to decide what to do and how to do it, and constantly making those high-stakes decisions is exhausting.

Moreover, without systems, every team member will make these moment-by-moment decisions in their own way. This will create conflict and mistakes. Steps will get skipped, and balls will get dropped. This is how burnout begins; you never get a day, or even an *hour*, off. So your life is chaotic—and the client experience is uneven at best.

Chaos is not scalable. Systems are. They create consistency, transparency, efficiency, and ease. They give you and your team the freedom to focus, to be creative, to build relationships. They free you from reinventing the wheel, allowing you to perfect it instead.

Systems also make recruitment easier and more effective. As other agents see your results and talk with members of your team, they'll be impressed. Remember, they, too, are stuck on that next-deal hamster wheel; chances are they're longing for systems, too, even if they don't yet know it. As a result, you'll attract better candidates and be able to pick and choose.

And when new team members do sign on, they'll get up to speed quicker. On day one, they can study your playbook and not only contribute, but do so in a way that maintains your quality standards. When team members leave, as some inevitably will, their knowledge won't walk out the door with them—it remains embedded in your systems.

Process also enables team members to step in for one another when needed. For example, Dana's team creates a cheat sheet for every listing, with information such as the lockbox and alarm codes, any major issues with the house, who the neighbors are, where the schools are located, and more. Thanks to this cheat sheet, any team member can run an open house or a showing at any time, and they'll be able to answer the most common questions immediately even if it's their first time at the property.

Dana doesn't even have to nag anyone to do this. It's a self-correcting process because if someone has to run an open house without a cheat sheet, the group chat blows up with questions. That annoys everyone, especially the agent who needed that time off—the same one who should have made the cheat sheet. The value of the process is self-evident.

The Eight Core Real Estate Systems

Now that you understand the power of systems, let's look at the eight systems every real estate business needs.

1: CRM (Client Relationship Manager)

This is the system for cultivating relationships on a consistent basis, which is the core of your business. Think of it as your to-do list, your business plan, your coach, and your database—all rolled into one. There are three major things your team must do to use your CRM right.

#1: Get the right people in, organized, grouped, and tagged in the right way.

Four groups of people belong in your CRM: current clients, past clients, leads, and your circle of influence (people who you have a relationship with but aren't leads, who should become leads if and when they start thinking of buying or selling). Make sure you have good contact information—especially phone numbers—and notes to remind you who each person is, how you know them, and what you should remember about them. Use tags to label important characteristics, like the neighborhood they live in or the value of their current home.

#2: Get everyone set up on a contact plan.

The only people who belong in your CRM are the ones with whom you intend to cultivate an ongoing relationship. That means someone on your team is picking up the phone and calling them every three months, *at minimum*. Not to sell or even talk about real estate, but just to catch up. *How are things going? How are the kids, the dog, the job?* That's what it takes to build a relationship. Assign contacts to your agents and set up reminders to make those calls.

#3: On a daily basis, do what your CRM says.

If you set up those tasks and reminders properly, your CRM becomes your automatic to-do list. Every day, you and your agents should dedicate at least an hour to doing all the things on the list, especially making those phone calls. They won't generate immediate sales—that's not the point. What they do is build and maintain relationships, so that when those people are ready to buy or sell, you'll be the first person they reach out to.

2: Leads

When a lead comes in, what do you do? How do you decide who gets to pursue that lead, and how will you ensure that they do so in the most effective way possible, to maximize the chance of getting hired and minimize the chance of wasting time on a dead end?

First, let's examine the question of how to distribute leads. This first came up when we discussed team structure in Chapter 5, because the answer depends on how you define your agents' roles. If all your agents are generalists, your process will be different than if they specialize in client type, geographic area, property type, or price point. Either way, the way you distribute leads *must* be transparent, logical, and consistent. Otherwise, you will foster uncertainty, resentment, and toxic competition among your agents.

That doesn't mean there's only one right answer, or that your process has to stay the same forever. We already mentioned that Dana's agents specialize in buyers or sellers, but they also used to specialize by price point as well. Listings that came in under $1 million went to one agent, $1 million to $2 million to another, $2 million to $3 million to another, and so on. Eventually, Dana switched to a rotating system, where agents take turns in each price bracket. This means no one gets stuck with all the lower-value listings, and it's simple to decide who gets a lead—Dana just looks at the property value and checks the list to see who is up next in that price range.

Now, what happens once the lead has been assigned? This, too, needs to be spelled out in black and white, because there are a lot of tasks to do and perhaps multiple people involved in them. Who will enter the lead into the database, or update their profile if they're already in it? When should the agent follow up, and what should they say? Who prepares the contract, and when does the agent present it to the lead? If you go on a listing appointment, who prepares the materials, and what should they include?

Most agents have never considered turning these questions into a repeatable system that can be learned by new team members. You might think it's better to just let your agents do things their way, but that's not real teamwork. If you're going to deliver a consistent client experience, and if you're going to ask your administrative staff to support multiple agents, the agents can't all be doing different things. Pick one path and mark it out clearly, with written guidelines and checklists, and if it needs to evolve over time, that's okay (more on that in Chapter 10).

3: Buyers

How does your team take a client from signing the buyer's agency agreement to signing the closing documents on a house? This is a whole set of processes, including:

- Getting to know buyers and introducing them to the area

- Picking properties and communicating about them
- Conducting showings
- Advising the buyer during the choice process
- Reviewing property disclosures
- Discussing offer price and terms
- Writing and delivering an offer
- Managing negotiations and inspections
- Coordinating with mortgage, escrow, and title professionals
- Closing the escrow
- Following up after closing
- And everything in between

Each of those items involves multiple tasks and decisions, so you can see how much room there is for variation—and for errors. To avoid that, you need to lay out all the details, even down to the specific questions you ask in your first meeting.

For example, Dana's buyer process begins with a two-hour tour of her market area. During this tour, the agent asks carefully predetermined questions that help sculpt a wish list, and all the information then goes into the database: favorite neighborhoods, preferred architectural styles, space needs, desired amenities, family size and lifestyle, and many more criteria. Having a standardized process ensures that every buyer gets a similar experience—a thorough one that captures all their needs and minimizes the time wasted considering properties that aren't a good fit.

4: Sellers

Now, how do you get a seller from listing agreement to sold? Just like the buyer side of the business, the seller side needs its own system. That includes:

- Getting to know the seller to understand their goals and timeline

- Setting the initial list price and crafting the marketing plan
- Preparing the house for sale (cleanup, repairs, staging, photography, etc.)
- Completing the property disclosures
- Creating a compelling listing and marketing it
- Scheduling, advertising the property, and running an open house and brokers' tour
- Receiving offers and discussing them with the seller
- Negotiating and accepting offers
- Managing the title and escrow process
- Transferring the property to the new owners
- And more

It's tempting to take some of these steps for granted, but that's how misunderstandings and mistakes happen. If you want to be able to trust your agents to take care of clients as well as you would, you need absolutely everything to be spelled out for them.

5: Marketing

We'll explore marketing in depth in Chapter 9. For now, we'll just say that most real estate marketing is ineffective precisely because it's not systematic. Just like everything else in your business, your marketing decisions should be strategic and planned, and you should have a repeatable process for making those decisions.

6: Transactions

How do you manage a transaction once a property is under contract? There are a lot of moving pieces and people involved at this phase, so it's critical to make sure the right things get done at the right time. Here are some processes to nail down:

- Facilitating communication between the buyer and seller
- Managing inspections and responding to the results

- Conducting appraisals and finalizing the loan process with the lenders
- Ensuring the title transfers properly from the seller to the buyer
- Preparing the property for transfer, including cleaning, repairs, utilities, etc.
- Ensuring the closing goes smoothly
- Sending thank you gifts and collecting feedback

These processes are especially critical because they determine how the final phase of the client's experience goes, which determines how they'll remember your team and whether they use you again or refer people to you in the future. The smoother you can make the transaction experience, the easier it will be to build your repeat and referral pipeline.

7: Finances

You'll learn more about managing your numbers in Chapter 11, but it should be obvious already that this is incredibly important. Other people's livelihoods depend on you, and it's your job to make sure the business stays financially sound. To do that, you need a set of processes to handle all the money-related tasks, including:

- Budgeting for future expenses
- Accounting for all revenue and costs
- Paying payroll
- Paying bills from vendors
- Keeping your insurance current
- Choosing and managing benefit plans
- Analyzing financial performance of the business

Automate these tasks as much as possible so you don't fall behind or let things slip through the cracks. Timeliness is important, and not just for paying other people. If you don't keep up, you can't know how your business is actually performing in the present, which makes it hard to make good management and spending decisions.

8: Communication

How does your team stay in touch, both internally and externally? You need clear processes that specify how to handle different types of communication, including what medium to use (call, text, email, video call), expected response times, who to copy, and how to record the communication in the appropriate log. Your processes should address communications with:

- Active clients
- Leads
- Past clients
- Teammates
- Team leader
- Vendors
- Other agents

In addition to actually getting things done, internal communication builds culture, and external communication builds brand. That's why it's so crucial to have standard procedures and make sure everyone follows them. Consistency in your communications will support a strong culture and brand.

How to Build Your Systems

Initially, the idea of creating systems may seem intimidating, as if you'll require code jockeys and MBAs. But relax: at its heart, any system is essentially a series of instructions, checklists, and calendars. In fact, some agents and teams still rely on paper for their systems, although most use project management software.

Think about systems as your equivalent to the checklists that pilots run through before a flight. On any given day, they could remember most of the items without a list, but *most* just isn't good enough—that's how planes go down. Your team, like that pilot, needs to do it *all*, never omitting *anything*, every single time.

And while you may not have to worry about crashing a plane, skipping or screwing up even one step could have major consequences. For starters, you could lose a client, who is sure to tell neighbors and acquaintances about their poor experience. Even more seriously, you could open yourself or your broker up to a lawsuit. And in a team setting, a mistake made by one member can affect everyone.

For example, a listing contract is supposed to start when the home is listed in the MLS. But what if the agent accidentally wrote a contract to begin the day they first met the client, which was forty-two days before the listing actually went up? Well, now instead of ninety days, they only have thirty-eight to sell the home before the seller can back out of the relationship and switch agents with no penalty.

Mistakes like this happen all the time in real estate, but they shouldn't. If you want to build a successful team, you can't afford to tolerate them. Thankfully, they're easy to prevent with robust systems.

The first key to building those systems is to get a systems-oriented person on the team. If you're the rainmaker, systems shouldn't be your responsibility. They will inevitably get pushed to the bottom of the list because selling will always be your top priority. Plus, let's be honest—you probably don't have the mindset or skills of a systems-builder. If you did, you would already have systems in place.

You need someone whose *primary* job is to build and maintain your business systems—someone who obsesses over process as much as the rainmaker obsesses over sales. This can be a consultant or a full member of the team, like your operations director or office manager. Only when this stuff becomes someone's first responsibility will it actually get done.

Even then, you won't have all the systems you need overnight. Every single task in your business needs a carefully crafted, documented process, and that takes time. Don't let that intimidate you into giving up on the whole thing. Just break it down into manageable steps. If you can turn just one workflow per week into a checklist, in a year you'll have well over forty checklists.

That's huge progress. Each checklist saves your team from mistakes and inefficiencies, so bit by bit you're saving time, reducing stress, and improving the client experience. The more processes you create, the more value you'll see in them, and the more momentum this whole endeavor will gain.

Now let's fast-forward to a time when those checklists have all been created, and your team has all its systems in place. When you hit that milestone, you face a new challenge: revising your processes continuously.

After every deal, sit down and perform an audit. What worked? What didn't? What's missing from the checklist, and what's wrong on it? Could it be better in any way?

You should lead this process, but you can't do it alone. The whole team needs to be involved because they're the ones actually using the systems every day. Empower everyone to provide feedback, make suggestions, and even create new processes when they're needed. Not only will the entire team benefit from different viewpoints, but you'll also earn buy-in by demonstrating that you value everybody's input.

Once you've developed systems, it's important to hold all team members accountable for using them. Now, that doesn't mean you should look over their shoulders and micromanage—that will just drive everybody nuts. No, all you need to do is stay aware of how people are performing. When people don't use the systems, there will be noticeable mistakes.

Don't just remedy the mistakes. Find out whether they happened because the process was flawed or because someone didn't follow the process. If it's the former, fix the process, or the same mistake will happen again and again (more on this in Chapter 10). If it's the latter, keep an eye out—someone who chronically resists using your systems is not a good fit for your team.

There will be rare circumstances in which the team, or one member, feels genuinely compelled to go off-process. This should be a big deal, a team decision. On Dana's team, if you want to go off-process, you have to ask the team and justify the request, because it's bound to affect other people.

It's also important not to let emotions derail your systems. For example, one of Steve's clients has a system that includes a pre-listing Zoom call. This prevents the team from going out on listing appointments until they've had a chance to determine whether they have a real shot at the listing. Recently, a new partner joined him, and when a lead came in, he was so excited that he booked the listing appointment without first doing the call.

The partners put in all the work to prepare for the appointment and give the presentation, only to realize afterward that they were never the favorite to win the listing. They never had a chance. It was all a waste of time and effort, and it could have been avoided if the new partner had followed the process. This is what happens when you let hope or fear override the system.

In the end, building and maintaining systems isn't that hard. They actually make your life easier, often immediately. You can't achieve sustainable success—solo or as a team—without them. Agents find endless excuses not to do it, but all the barriers are mental.

Time. You may think you don't have time to build systems, but in reality, you don't have time *not* to. When they're in place, your systems will save you countless hours—more and more as your team grows. If you don't make time to create them now, you're just digging yourself deeper into a hole of endless busy-ness.

Overconfidence. You think you don't need to write it down because you know it all. Don't kid yourself—there's more to do than any one person can keep track of. If your team is to consistently provide a great client experience, everyone needs absolute clarity on what to do, when, and how. Only documented systems can provide that.

Pride. Process, shmocess. All these checklists and calendars feel like menial, boring stuff that's beneath you . . . but actually, system-building is the most important, productive thing you can do for your business. Yes, even more important than bringing in leads. What good are leads if you can't reliably give them a great experience and keep them coming back?

Laziness. You grasp the importance of systems, and you want the outcome. You just don't want to do the work. That's fine—make it someone else's job. Just make sure the work gets done.

Habit. You're used to winging it, and you've gotten away with it for a long time because you're quick on your feet. But that only takes you so far. Once you start building a team, winging it is not going to work anymore.

In the end, if you're serious about building a team that will outlast you and become a saleable asset, you can't afford *not* to have systems. They are the only way to scale up successfully. They'll enable your team to work as one sleek unit, fulfilling your promise to clients. And they allow you to trust your team, so you can let go and stop trying to do everything.

Chapter 8

PEOPLE

Here's a story we've seen play out a thousand times.

You have enough people on your team—barely. When everybody's operating at full throttle, you can just about cover your bases, but it's stressful. Truth be told, you could use another person, but you're not sure you can afford one.

Then somebody quits out of nowhere, and all hell breaks loose. Everybody on the team is overwhelmed. You get flashbacks to your pre-team days, when you were on your phone 24-7-365 and had no life whatsoever. You need to hire a new person, and you need to do it now.

Clearly, this is incredibly stressful. You don't have time to deal with hiring and onboarding; you're too busy keeping all the plates spinning for your clients. Besides, you don't have much experience hiring, so you're not exactly sure how to do it right.

Because you don't have hiring materials or processes set up, you're forced to wing it. You end up hiring a friend of a friend because she was recommended to you. Hey, you got along with her during the interview. She seemed excited about the opportunity and was willing to accept any conditions.

That was a few weeks ago, and it's now clear that things aren't working out as you had hoped. Your new hire is busy, but not with the right things. She's nice and likable, but she's not a good fit with your team's culture. She's not producing the results you care about—and she's costing you money.

Not all of this is her fault. She doesn't have all the skills the job requires, and nobody has time to train her. As a result, you feel obliged to micromanage her to avert serious errors. Three months later, she quits, and you have to go through all this again.

Make no mistake: the greatest challenge in building a team is finding and keeping the right people. If you don't get this right, nothing else matters.

And in order to hire and retain the right people, you'll need to have a system in place, just as you do for every other part of your business. The idea of the system is to eliminate as much gray as possible—to make everything black and white, so you and the entire team are on the same page with no room for misinterpretation. On a new hire's first day, they should have a playbook that spells out everything: schedules, responsibilities, expectations, and every other detail about their role.

When you have good people systems in place, you'll attract higher-quality team members, and you'll set them up to succeed. Without systems, you'll find yourself attracting wounded birds and setting them up for failure. Remember, you want to attract people who make the team better, not people who will contribute to the chaos. This chapter will show you how.

Define the Role

Every single role on your team needs a job description—a *detailed* one. Not just a title or a one-paragraph summary. Not even a one-page overview is really enough. A complete job description contains much more than that because it needs to accomplish several things:

- Attract the right person, with the right skills and qualities for the role
- Make sure the new hire understands what they're getting into—what's expected of *them* and what they can expect from *you*—to head off surprises and disappointments
- Set them up for success in their work
- Create clear standards for evaluating their performance

Laying all this out in advance vastly reduces the chances of a bad hire, but few teams bother to do this. Dana often gets calls from other team leaders saying they've just hired someone—can she send over a job description the team can apply to the newbie? Talk about backward!

So what's in a proper job description? This list should provide a good start.

Basic information. This includes the job title, direct supervisor, and work schedule, as well as the employment classification (part-time, full-time, or independent contractor) and the compensation and benefits offered. It should also include the purpose of the role: a brief statement about why the role exists.

Experience and education. What kind of training and experience is required to succeed in the role? This is typically the least important thing, especially experience in real estate. You can teach real estate—it's not that complicated. However, there may be some business management roles that require a certain type of degree, special certifications, or experience in a particular field.

For example, Steve helped hire a chief operating officer for a real estate team that needed someone who could create and implement processes. One candidate had worked on big real estate teams, while the other was from Goldman Sachs. Despite having no real estate experience, the Goldman Sachs candidate was a more strategic thinker and was better able to innovate and figure out what truly needed doing (as opposed to simply relying on past experience). Steve advised the team to overlook the lack of real estate experience and hire this candidate.

Skills. Include all specific technical and soft skills required to succeed in the role. Even if you think a particular skill is a given, be sure to include it. (Dana once hired an executive assistant who turned out to be uncomfortable answering the phone. Talk about a bad fit!) Soft skill examples include the ability to think on your feet; organization and attention to detail; comfort with technology; and good verbal and written communication skills.

Values and personality. Share your team's values. Describe the exact type of person you want to see in the role in terms of attitude and drive.

Responsibilities and tasks. What do you expect the person who fills this role to do every day? Every week? Every month? Don't be afraid to go into great detail here. Otherwise, they'll have to guess, and their thinking may not line up with yours.

Key performance indicators. How will you judge whether they're doing a good job? What metrics will you track? Again, be specific. This prevents confusion and conflict in the future.

An assignment. Ask all candidates to include a cover letter on why they want the position and why they think they would be a good fit. You'll be amazed at how many people fail this very first request, which will help you weed them out.

A job description should be a living document. Anytime a role turns over or evolves, refine the job description. Whenever a hire doesn't work out, look back and see if you can adjust the job description to help prevent that kind of mismatch again. Indeed, every year, Dana has her team check their job descriptions and make any necessary updates.

Find the Right Person

Once you've created a thorough job description, you have to put the word out, both organically and online. There is no magic formula here. Just post your offer in all the usual places: Indeed, LinkedIn, Wizehire, Craigslist, ZipRecruiter, etc.

Then clean your glasses, because you're going to read resumes. Lots and lots of resumes. You could hire an outside consultant to help you through this process, but that's expensive, and in our experience, it doesn't provide a better result than doing the work on your own.

Remember the mad rush we described early in the chapter, when being in a hurry to hire created a bad situation? It's important to take your time during this process. Hiring well is a pain in the neck. It requires effort and diligence. Work your way through it. Don't rush, don't settle.

And *always* check references. If a reference doesn't have any comments . . . well, that's a comment.

It's a good idea to have multiple team members interview candidates. After all, the new hire needs to work well with everybody else on the team, not just you. Moreover, somebody else may spot a red flag that you miss. Dana usually prefers to do the final interview, trusting other members of her team to do the initial vetting.

During the interview, the candidate should do most of the talking. Many interviewers talk too much, usually out of nervousness. But as long as you're talking, you're not learning about the candidate. Don't spend all this valuable time selling *them* on your team—they need to be selling *you*. Make sure they truly understand the role, and watch out for signs that they haven't done their homework. If they seem unaware of things that are clearly spelled out in the job description or on your website, they aren't serious about this opportunity.

Make it a goal to interview at least ten people for each position. That may seem like a lot, but there are no shortcuts when you're looking for the best. Thorough interviewing is how you learn what's out there, what people can and can't do. It's also how you build a deep bench; you may encounter a candidate who's not quite right for your current opening but will be perfect for another one later.

As we mentioned earlier, don't overvalue real estate experience when evaluating candidates. You can teach real estate quickly. What you *can't* teach, on the other hand, is intelligence, attitude, values, desire, and work ethic. You can't put a fire in anyone's belly. The candidate has to bring all that to the table.

You also don't want to have to teach core technical skills for the role, whatever those may be—things like project management, software skills, budgeting, spreadsheets, etc. While there's a break-in period for any new hire, as we've discussed, you can't afford to have employees learning crucial skills like these on the job.

In addition to competence, remember to consider the candidate's values and personality. Are they friendly? Will your team and clients enjoy working with them? Are they a good fit for your culture? Are they a hand-up person, always asking how they can contribute? Or are they a hand-out person, asking what they'll get from the position? While you pride your team on being a great working environment, keep in mind that you're not hiring people to take care of them. No, you're hiring them to put them in a position to contribute to the team's success.

One good way to identify team-oriented people is to use a reputable personality test, like the Myers-Briggs® or DISC test. These are common in corporate hiring processes, and for good reason. They are designed to reveal characteristics that show how well someone will fit with the team and with a specific role, which can save you from big hiring mistakes.

Always close interviews with this straightforward request: "Tell me why I should hire you."

Listen carefully to their answer. Can the candidate respond in a precise, intelligent way? You'll be surprised at how many cannot. As they answer, evaluate whether they see themselves as a contributor to the team.

It's smart to give a simple assignment at the end of the interview—nothing extraordinary or taxing, just something that can be done quickly. A bit of research on your market, for example. This is another easy way to let candidates eliminate themselves, because believe it or not, most won't do the extra work. That will tell you everything you need to know about their desire for the position and their follow-through.

If possible, have the top candidates do a trial run of some kind. For example, you might ask them to spend a day observing and interacting with the team.

Years ago, Dana had a stager observe for a day in this manner. The candidate, who was excellent, came back and said the lead stager was never going to give her the freedom and control she wanted, so it wasn't a good fit. That was great—Dana avoided hiring the wrong person and adjusted the interview process going forward.

You might even consider asking people to do a ninety-day trial before the relationship is finalized. This kind of contract makes it easier to part ways if things don't work out, and it incentivizes the new hire to get up to speed quickly and prove their value to the team.

Develop Your Players

The number one challenge in building a team is attracting the right people. The number two challenge is developing the talent that you hire. The idea that your new hires are going to produce at the level you want with little or no guidance or accountability is extremely naive. Productivity does not happen by accident.

And yet, the real estate business is notorious for throwing people in the deep end and waiting to see if they figure it out. This only sets people up for failure, which leads to high turnover, which—as we've said before—is expensive, stressful, and demoralizing. As an employer, that turnover will leave you gun-shy. You'll find it tempting to avoid hiring and revert to just doing everything yourself—which will make it impossible to get your life back, and that's one of your main reasons for creating a team, right?

So instead of leaving everyone to fend for themselves, develop your team members. Train them to do the job the way you need it done, and build systems to keep everyone on the same page. This requires both a well-thought-out process and time.

It starts with clear expectations and consequences in writing. That's why your team playbook and job descriptions are so critical. They should map out everything each person needs to do to be a productive member of your team, as well as what will happen if they don't. Everything should be black and white, with no room for confusion or misinterpretation. Gray is the enemy.

Still, it's not enough to just hand a new hire a bunch of documents explaining their role and send them off. You need to walk them through these expectations, answer their questions, and teach them the skills they need. This training should include, at a minimum:

1. What you want each agent to focus on
2. How they block their time
3. How they use their CRM
4. What they do each day
5. How they track what they do
6. How they improve their sales skills
7. How you measure and evaluate their progress
8. Team culture, mindset, and attitude

Remember, agents will come to you with an independent-contractor mindset. They're used to coming and going as they please and doing things their way. That does *not* work in a team setting. You're trying to replace that mindset and those habits with true teamwork, and that takes both time and repetition. That's why training must be consistent and systematic, not haphazard.

Without an emphasis on training and accountability, you can't expect your agents to meet your production standards. Ultimately, this means you can't expect to achieve your goals, because team production—not your production alone—determines the success of the team. Most teams fall incredibly short of the mark when it comes to player development, so this is an opportunity for drastic improvement.

In addition to training, you also need systems to keep everyone aligned with each other and on track with their individual tasks and goals.

For example, Dana has a simple daily communication system with her assistant. They have a phone call first thing every morning to get aligned on the schedule, agenda, and key goals for the day. At the end of the day, Dana's assistant emails her about calendar changes, questions, and unresolved inbox items, and Dana has to respond before she goes offline for the evening. With her team, the communication system is a weekly meeting every Monday morning, featuring the same agenda each week: a core value highlight, the team calendar, escrows and closings, the CEO's market update, gratitude, marketing, events, and announcements.

Rather than phone calls, video calls, or email, your team may use project management software to stay aligned on what's happening. There are many ways to do it; what matters is having a system and sticking with it. The format, cadence, and content of your communication should be consistent.

You'll also need a system for performance reviews (more on this in Chapter 12). Dana conducts them twice a year, with the midyear review a progress check-in and the year-end review focused on compensation and bonuses. On her team, agents evaluate themselves in writing; Dana responds in writing; and then they meet to discuss.

As with communication, what's important to the review process is consistency. Everyone should know exactly when it's going to happen, what will happen, and what the possible outcomes are. What they're being evaluated on should line up with what their job description asks of them, as well as the values and principles that guide the entire team. Performance evaluations have high stakes—you're talking about people's livelihoods here. Consistency is the key to making the process fair and predictable.

Once again, strong processes create true teamwork. Without them, the only way to get the work done right is to micromanage, which annoys everyone—especially the smartest and strongest on your team. It also trains people to rely on you for constant instruction, which makes your workload overwhelming. And aren't you trying to get your life back? Great systems allow your team members to take ownership of their roles, so you don't have to.

Fire Fast

Let's face it: firing people is not something anybody takes pleasure in. But when you sign on to be the leader of a business, it's a responsibility to handle as well as you can.

Steve's long coaching career has taught him two important lessons in this area:

1. If you're talking about the same team member every week on your coaching call, that person is not working out.
2. Things rarely get better with a problem employee.

We tend to give people far too many chances, accept far too much poor performance, and put up with bad hires for far too long. But nothing happens in a vacuum; a subpar employee is constantly damaging the entire team, through errors of commission or omission. At some point, it will be your job to repair the damage to spirit and morale.

Robert Reffkin, CEO of Compass, uses what he calls the Keeper Test. If someone on your team came to you and said they were leaving, would you fight to keep them? Look at each person on your team, and if the answer is no, let them go ASAP.

Interestingly, rainmakers are the *worst* at terminations. They are, after all, people people. They get along with everybody and don't like hurting anybody.

For this reason, it's best to keep yourself out of the firing mix if possible. Make it someone else's job to terminate people—your HR director or chief of staff, whoever is in charge of personnel stuff. If you don't yet have someone like that on your team, the job will have to fall to you . . . and the danger is that you'll avoid it instead of doing it when it really needs to be done.

It helps immensely to have a clear process for this as well. Lay out in writing all the possible grounds for termination, as well as how many warnings you'll give someone before firing them. Follow the language in your employment contract, and make sure every team member is fully aware of these policies.

When you have to implement them, document everything thoroughly. Keep records of exactly what happened, what was said, and when—and make sure your warnings are in writing. Otherwise, you risk leaving yourself open to a lawsuit.

You should also create an "offboarding" process, which is simply a checklist to follow whenever someone leaves the team. For example, conduct a scripted exit interview and collect keys, credit cards, playbooks, and other team assets. Change any network passwords they had access to, and delete their accounts.

This last one is especially important and often overlooked; in all industries, departing team members are a major source of data breaches. Some sabotage their former employers' systems for revenge, while others take proprietary information along to their next job. Whatever the case, you can mitigate that risk with a few keystrokes.

Stay Prepared to Hire

Are you +1, neutral, or –1?

Most real estate teams are operating at a deficit—they never have quite enough people. That means hiring is always reactionary, not proactive.

If you only go into hiring mode when you're desperate and crunched for time, you will rush the process. You won't take the time necessary to create a structure, and you'll be more likely to settle for somebody who's just okay rather than holding out for the perfect fit.

For these reasons, we advise teams to try to stay at +1. Have someone on the bench. We guarantee you're going to lose team members unexpectedly, whether to a temporary illness or to a sudden departure. If you have no bench, you'll find yourself at a major disadvantage in those moments. You and all remaining team members will see your quality of life suffer as you scramble to fill gaps.

Look at it this way: if your favorite pro sports team suffered an injury and had no one on the bench, ready to step in, you'd be justifiably furious. Don't make this mistake.

Another common problem is budgeting for a new hire. Team leaders seldom have money set aside for this purpose, and that's a mistake. The reality is that financially, you must be ready to support a position for up to six months while a newbie comes up to speed. You can't expect them to get amazing results and pay for themselves right away. That's wishful thinking. If you hire first and assume you'll figure out the pay later, you're starting the relationship on a rocky footing and setting up both the new hire and the overall team for failure.

In the end, one thread connects everything: *think it through.*

HR is about eliminating chaos and confusion. It's about answering everyone's questions. The way to find the right people is to put a process in place. You can't really know who you have until they're in the job, but a strong process can go a long way toward eliminating the worst fits.

The trouble is, most team leaders don't do any of this vetting. In most cases, they don't even realize they need it. And even if they did know, they don't have time (that is, they have failed to set aside the time) to do the up-front work that makes for quality hires. They're stuck in that chasing-what's-next mentality that marks even successful agents—always rushed, always behind the eight ball.

But if you're going to build a real team, a lasting business that has transferable value and is more than just your name on a sign, it's absolutely necessary to create a consistent, repeatable process for hiring, training, managing, and firing people.

Chapter 9

MARKETING

There was this big team. And we mean *big*—this team did three hundred deals a year and had a lock on the top spot in its core markets.

Well, this team decided to do an aggressive mailing program covering not only those core markets, in which it enjoyed so much success, but also surrounding markets. The idea was to leverage the team's core-market competitive edge to gain share in other markets. In two years, the team spent $200,000 in mailing to those other fringe markets. After all that time and all that spending, do you want to know how much new business they won?

Zero. That's right: $200,000 in marketing got the team no new business whatsoever. Unsurprisingly, the disastrous program was terminated.

What happened here?

The team leader did something far too many agents are guilty of: impulsive marketing. Agents see other teams or solo agents doing some marketing activity. *That looks nice*, they think, or *That seems like a good idea*. Then they go out and copy the tactics without thinking them through strategically.

Here's the dirty little secret: the agent you're imitating is probably copying someone else, who is copying someone else, and so on. They don't know some big marketing secret you don't. This is the blind leading the blind.

The result is wasted resources and missed opportunities. It's common in small-business marketing, and it's very common in the real estate industry. You don't know how to measure your results, so you don't know what works and what doesn't, and you end up wasting time and effort on useless marketing. Naturally, this also means you're not investing enough in *effective* marketing.

Worse, your brand becomes jumbled and diluted because you didn't create your marketing assets strategically, with strict adherence to your brand guidelines. Incoherent brands aren't memorable, and they don't build trust among consumers. That's a major problem, because the primary job of marketing in real estate is to build awareness and relationships. This is a long-term process that must be designed with intention.

Unfortunately, most agents do the exact opposite: they wing their marketing and expect it to generate short-term results. In this chapter, you'll learn why that's so dangerous, and what to do instead.

What Marketing Is Really For

First, let's clear one thing up: marketing and branding are not the same thing. Your brand is your *emotional promise* to the client. Think back to Chapter 4: your brand is your public identity as a team. It's what you stand for, what you value, how you do business. Think of Four Seasons versus Walmart. These are two very different brands that stand for different things—and both are valid and successful. Both deliver on their promises, which happen to be quite different.

If your brand is your public identity, marketing is the *tactical execution* of your brand. It's the sum total of the things you say and do in public to express that identity. Marketing isn't merely your website, your brochures, your ads, business cards, etc. It also encompasses everything else you do—the events you attend, the gifts you give clients, even (*especially*) the way you conduct business day-to-day.

There is a marketing model called AIDA that when used effectively impacts your prospective clients' decision-making process in your favor. Each letter stands for one of the four steps a person goes through subconsciously, and in many cases consciously, to become your client.

- **Awareness**: Have they even heard of you?
- **Information**: Do they know what you do?
- **Decision**: Are you their favorite?
- **Action**: Are they going to actually work with you?

AIDA applies to all industries, but real estate is different from retail, which is the source of most of the marketing you see day-to-day. In retail, an enormous percentage of marketing is oriented toward the last step, Action. That's the case when, for example, you step into the grocery store and see 70 percent off oranges or a buy-one-get-one offer on cookies next to the cash register. The store is trying to get you to buy things you weren't planning to buy when you walked in.

Need we point out that real estate doesn't work that way? A home is not an impulse buy. You have no control over when someone is ready to buy or sell. No marketing is going to convince someone to take that action if they didn't already plan to do so.

This industry calls for a different approach. The goal of your marketing is to make your team the first to come to mind when a potential client *does* decide it's time to buy or sell. Here's another way to view it: at any given time, only 3–5 percent of all homeowners are selling. That means 95–97 percent of the people who see your marketing aren't ready to act, and nothing—*nothing*—you say or do will change that.

So don't waste time and money trying. Instead, focus on building awareness, interest, and desire. If people know your name, understand what you do, and feel positive about you, you'll be well positioned when the time comes for them to make a move.

That kind of marketing is a long-term game. We need to stress this, because we've seen so many agents and teams fail to grasp it: you will *not* get a thirty-day return on your marketing investments. It makes no sense to expect this; it's not how the business works. Your marketing efforts will pay off over the course of one to three years.

That means you need a strategic plan. Without a plan, you'll give in to impulse, like the team that spent $200,000 for nothing. You'll try one thing, not see immediate results, assume it's not working, and then scrap it and try something else. This cycle will repeat itself over and over.

Without a plan, you'll do some marketing when you've got some budget to throw at it. When you don't, you'll neglect it. Moreover, you'll forget about marketing when business is booming and you're crazy busy. After all, who needs marketing when clients are throwing themselves at you? But when business is slow, you'll panic about your lack of marketing and grab the first idea that comes along, whether it makes sense for your team or not.

The result will be big peaks and valleys in both your revenue and your marketing spend. This isn't good for your balance sheet—or your sanity. So let's dig into how your team can approach real estate marketing the smart way.

Stop Destroying Your Brand

The first step toward effective marketing is a complete marketing audit. This is just what it sounds like. Gather all the marketing collateral you use: website, brochures, signs, mailers, ads, business cards, listing presentations, swag bags, the works. If it's digital, print it out.

Now, pin it all up on a wall as a collection, study it, and ask yourself some hard questions.

Does it look like one brand?
Look closely at the details: fonts, colors, graphics, images, and language. Are they consistent? Probably not always, unless you've had clear brand guidelines in place for several years already. Chances are you'll see a great deal of "marketing creep," where these details shift little by little depending on when something was made and who made it. These inconsistencies undermine your brand's recognizability and the strength of its message.

Do your materials focus on your team, rather than you as an individual?
We've discussed how a high-performing team can't simply rely on its leader's reputation. There should be plenty of "we" in both your language and pictures. Setting expectations is a key component of marketing, and you want to communicate the message that clients will be working with the team, not just with you. Your materials should explain the roles of all team members and, even more importantly, the *value* of working with a team.

Do your materials reflect the brand you've decided on?
Back in Chapter 4, we advised you to hire a brand consultant to help you choose the colors, fonts, imagery, and language

that would embody your team's public identity. Do your marketing materials reflect those choices? You should be able to look at them and think, *Yes, this is who we really are.*

Here's a subtle example. Remember Carey, whose story we told in the introduction? Her tagline is "Living beyond the four walls." When Jonathan was helping with a marketing audit, he removed all photos of interiors from her collateral. This may seem radical—real estate marketing without handsome interior photos?—but the shots distracted from, and even contradicted, the brand message.

Are your materials free from errors and sloppiness?
Typos, grammar mistakes, missing information, blurry photos, dead links—these little details can seriously detract from the effectiveness of your marketing. They send the message that your team isn't paying close attention and might let mistakes happen . . . and if it happens in your marketing, it probably happens in your deals too. No one wants that from the person handling their biggest personal asset. Think quality over quantity; you're better off putting in extra effort to make your collateral really sing, even if it means hiring a copy editor or proofreader.

As you answer these questions, compile a list of all the assets that need to be updated and the specific changes that need to be made. Get your team involved in this process; you probably won't spot all the problems yourself, and they can help you flag issues.

And of course, if you don't yet have the brand book we discussed in Chapter 4, now's the time to make it. This is where you'll set your brand guidelines in stone, delineating what to do and what *not* to do. It's critical that everyone on your team has access to these guidelines. If they don't, we guarantee they will continue creating and publishing material that dilutes your brand, and all the effort of this audit will go to waste. Brand guidelines are an insurance policy, just like the processes we explored in Chapter 7; they prevent people, including you, from making costly mistakes.

Once you've identified the problems in a thorough audit, it's time to make a plan to fix them. Start with digital materials; this is the low-hanging fruit because the changes are instant and cost nothing. Changing printed marketing collateral, on the other hand, requires more time and money. You'll want to form an action plan to use up existing materials, cycle them out, and replace them with updated versions.

As you make these changes, remember that good marketing is much more science than art. It's not impulsive—it's goal oriented. It's rational. It's *consistent.*

That's a word worth repeating. Consistency and quality are both more important than quantity. When your brand is consistent, you condition people to have certain expectations, which is exactly what you need your marketing to do.

Make a Strategic Plan

No more winging it—it's time to be proactive instead of reactive. Remember, reactive marketing doesn't work. It just turns your business into a roller coaster. Effective marketing is a long-term game, which is why you need to think well in advance.

So once your audit is complete, it's time to plan out all the ways you'll market your team: the ads, online content, events, sponsorships, and anything else you might spend resources on. This plan should span an entire year—yes, twelve whole months—and include budgets of both money and time. How big those budgets are isn't nearly as important as simply having a plan.

Here are ten tips for creating a strong marketing plan.

1. Get expert guidance.

We recommend working with a marketing expert to build your strategy. That could be your in-house marketing director, or if you don't have one, an outside consultant. Even if you have a background in marketing, you also have a lot of other responsibilities on your plate, and if you don't get help, this crucial work might not get done.

2. Commit in advance.

Once you've made a plan, commit to it by signing contracts, paying deposits, assigning tasks, and putting deadlines on the calendar. For example, Dana locks down the same ad spots in key publications every year, so consumers see her brand over and over in the same places. This is how you increase your brand awareness over time.

3. Measure what matters.

The biggest challenge in marketing is to figure out what's working. The only feedback most agents get is, "I see your name everywhere." That's nice to hear, of course, but face it: most of the folks who say it are people who already know you, so it doesn't mean much.

To know what's effective and what's a waste of time and money, you have to collect data. Start by asking *all* your leads how they heard about you—from Google, social media, an ad, a friend? If it was a person, find out who. This should be one of the first questions you ask, and you should track the responses in your CRM.

Next, pay attention to your website stats: overall traffic, how much time visitors spend there, and what they look at. Your website is your 24-7-365 salesperson, and these stats can tell you how well it's working and how you can improve it. That said, they can be tricky to track and interpret correctly, which is another good reason to work with a savvy marketing specialist.

4. Stick to your sweet spot.

Remember what you learned in Chapter 6: focus on your sweet spot. That $200,000 flop of a mailing campaign that we mentioned earlier failed because the team was mailing to an area where it was not dominant. Even in their core market, where they *are* number one, they have 10 percent market share at best. That means 90 percent of the business is there to be captured, largely from agents who only do one or two deals a year there.

You can see where we're going with this. The team had a great opportunity to grow in its home turf, where it enjoyed excellent brand recognition and plentiful referrals. Once you consider this, the idea of spending $200,000 in a futile effort to capture new territory is obviously a poor decision—the type of decision agents and teams make when they don't have a plan.

5. Nurture your existing client base.

If you're a rookie with a tiny (or even nonexistent) client database, you'll have to focus your marketing efforts on building brand awareness with the public and growing that database.

On the other hand, if you already have a large client base, you're better off focusing on them. Call former clients. Send them something. Stay in touch. Most agents spend more time marketing to strangers (which is very difficult) than they do marketing to their database. That's a mistake—just like marketing outside your sweet spot.

Once again, this marketing isn't about making them take action. It's about maintaining their awareness of your team and nurturing their relationship with you. Check in on them not to get something from them, but to show you care, and to stay top of mind so that when the time comes to move again, you'll be the first person they call.

6. Share knowledge.

You can't control markets or when someone decides to buy or sell, but you *can* control how informed the community is and whether they view you as a trusted expert. Position yourself as an expert by educating your audience about the market, as well as the buying and selling process. This builds trust by showing them not only that you know your stuff but also that you have their best interests at heart—you're sharing your insight openly rather than hoarding it for yourself.

For example, Dana's team publishes two blogs: one that's community focused and another that is business focused. Additionally, they regularly publish market insights that educate readers about local and national real estate trends. In addition to providing value for clients and prospects, this content helps generate website traffic and leads.

7. Show gratitude.

Build deep connections with the community by giving back. Get involved in a public, visible way by sponsoring local events and organizations, especially ones that matter most to your team. For example, if the local schools are a big draw in your area, become a vocal supporter and show that you care about the institutions that make your community strong. Sports teams, festivals, charities—there are endless ways to give back. Dana's team sponsors their city's holiday light display and attends the lighting ceremony, which is great fun and also keeps her team highly visible.

And of course, don't forget to show gratitude to your existing clients. Thank-you gifts for closings and referrals are the basics, but you can do more. One agent we know hand-delivers one-hundred-dollar holiday wreaths to two hundred past clients each year. Now, $20,000 is a lot of money, and those clients aren't going to call her wanting to sell in the next thirty days. But over the next three to five years, enough of them (not to mention those they refer) will do business with her to more than justify the expense.

Another agent has thrown a holiday party every year for more than a decade. These are marketing dollars well spent; their value compounds every year. Attendees roll in, and what do they have in common? This agent! This is incredibly powerful, as it creates an emotional experience the clients link to her, positioning her as a trusted advisor. Think of it this way: It's highly unlikely that someone will attend your party every year, then *not* do business with you when the time comes.

8. Be authentic.

There isn't one right answer in marketing. What's right for you is what's authentic—what feels natural and aligns with your brand. Authenticity is so important because it creates consistency. When it feels natural to do something, you won't have to struggle to make yourself do it over and over. And when your marketing choices come from an authentic place, they will align with and reinforce each other.

Think of it like a word-search puzzle: the answers come in many different formats—horizontal, vertical, diagonal, backward, forward—but each one stays in its lane. So pick your lane and stay in it. Build your network and your brand by simply doing things you like to do, and have your team do likewise. Maybe you take your dog to the local dog parks. Maybe you're in the community tennis league. Maybe you coach youth sports.

You'll make friends, connections, and eventually clients this way, and it will all be organic. By contrast, if you don't like dogs but you show up at the dog park every morning, it'll be obvious you're there to sell, and nobody respects that. Stay in your lane.

Authenticity is especially important for gifts. Most agents give closing and holiday gifts, but they often fail to have any emotional impact because they're just generic trinkets. They don't come from a place of genuinely knowing someone and nurturing a relationship with them. It's the thought that counts, and if you don't put any thought into your gifts, they count for nothing.

9. Involve your team.

Your team doesn't need to weigh in on every single marketing decision, but do bring them into the loop on some things. For example, take suggestions on the events and organizations your team sponsors, focusing on the ones where they have personal connections. Invite their participation in discussions about where and when to advertise. Have them review important marketing pieces before they go out.

By involving the team, you help them buy into and believe in the plan. This is crucial because it's one of the key benefits of their joining your team. Having them leverage team content that is aligned with the brand guidelines is a more effective branding strategy and win-win for the agent and the overall team.

10. Don't follow the pack.

Why pay for an ad that looks just like the other twenty right next to it? Why say the same things everyone else is saying? That won't make you stand out, so it's a waste of time and money. To be seen as an expert, you need a voice that's different from everyone else's.

Not long ago, when the market was red hot, Dana noticed that most agents were running "brag" ads. You know the type: *I sold this many homes! I did more volume than X, Y and Z!* Well, Dana saw all this zigging and decided to zag. Her team responded by putting out a quiet thank-you ad, simply telling clients and other stakeholders how grateful the team was for their business.

Don't get complacent. You must remain creative, always thinking of new ways to stand out while remaining true to your brand.

Do you think you can't afford to take the time for this kind of strategic planning? Well, we've got news: you can't afford *not* to. Marketing is a crucial component of any modern business—especially one as competitive as real estate.

Remember, you're building a team in order to create an organization that will be bigger than, and outlast, your name on the sign. Can you think of any small business that can thrive and grow without investing in marketing? Neither can we.

Your marketing efforts should be like a constant reminder. Don't fall into the trap of impulsive or ego-driven marketing splurges. Even if you do something only once a year, be sure to do it *every* year. Pace yourself. Be consistent. If you want to earn three transactions from a client spread over twenty years, you need to build a twenty-year relationship. Flash and gimmicks won't cut it—only consistent, authentic messaging will do the trick.

Chapter 10

CONTINUOUS IMPROVEMENT

Not long ago, an agent on Dana's team had a Sunday open house. When the day rolled around, the agent found, to her horror, that there were no Open House sign tags for the property. Nobody had created them. Naturally, she was ticked off.

When Dana found out, she was determined to get to the bottom of things. Someone forgot to create the sign tags, yes. But *why?* Because "Create sign tags for Open House" was not on the checklist. Naturally, then, step one was to *put* it on the checklist. Immediately.

That doesn't guarantee this will never happen again—after all, everyone still has to remember to *use* the checklist—but it goes a long way. The last-minute pain (as the agent desperately scrambled to create sign tags and make the open house in time) could have been avoided with an easy fix. Just imagine how many moments of stress and frustration will be silently saved in the future now that a repeat of this disaster has been prevented.

More importantly, look at your own business and add up all the time spent solving problems that never should have happened in the first place. Miscommunications, missteps, missing information—on most teams, they eat up a huge chunk of every week, if not every day. Virtually every agent and team we know is constantly putting out fires.

Life is a lot easier when you take the time to prevent them instead. Even when you're at your busiest, you must build in time to *learn* from mistakes, not just rectify them. In this chapter, you'll see how to improve your processes, celebrate successes, and anticipate what's coming down the line, even at the peak of your season.

Get Smarter Every Day

If you're not careful, real estate can be death by a thousand paper cuts. Every transaction involves countless details, and the little mistakes here and there make the difference between a great client experience and a mediocre one. Great experiences lead to repeat and referral business; mediocre ones don't.

So errors that seem small are actually a major roadblock to success. If you want to build a sustainable business without burning out, you've got to cut out these unforced errors anytime you come across one. The team should make fewer and fewer mistakes every week.

You can't make this happen by yourself, no matter how smart and experienced you may be. The industry, and indeed the world, is too complex; it moves too quickly for any one person to have eyes on everything.

After all, you're not in the field with your agents. You don't have an overview of everything they're seeing and doing. They're the ones with the most information about their clients, properties, and deals. At the same time, they don't always know what their fellow team members are doing, and they can't see the big picture of the market and industry the way you can.

That's why you have to harness the team's collective intelligence. You *all* have to share information and work together to identify and prevent problems.

Collective intelligence is one of the major advantages of being on a team. Each team member can learn from every deal, even those they're not directly involved in. They can pick up on best practices, learn common pitfalls to avoid, and generally benefit from the experience of others. That means each individual learns faster as part of the group than they would on their own.

And the more they learn, the more valuable they become as team members. Not only do their skills grow, but they also become adept at problem-solving instead of complaining or making the same mistakes repeatedly.

But if you don't incorporate that learning into your processes, it can walk out the door at any moment. This happens to real estate teams all the time. A star performer who carried the team suddenly leaves—maybe they decided they'd be better off on their own, or maybe life happened and they just had to move on. Either way, you're left in the lurch because you don't know how they did what they did, and neither does anyone else. Replacing them will be impossible.

That's why you have to continuously incorporate your team's learning into your documented processes, so it can be shared across the team and taught to new employees. That way, the knowledge becomes institutionalized—it stays in your business and contributes to its value. The goal is to create systems that allow anyone to step into a given role, follow established processes, and do the job right.

Build a Learning Process

Speaking of processes, learning itself should be a structured process of its own. Otherwise, it simply won't happen. One way to do this is to make it a standing agenda item in your weekly team meeting. (You do have a weekly meeting, right? If not, you need to institute one ASAP.)

When you tackle learning regularly, you solve problems cumulatively. Here's what to do:

- **Celebrate wins.** Remind the team of all the issues you've solved before—this will build confidence that you can solve the next one.
- **Analyze losses.** Examine the past week's mistakes and failures, and discuss how to prevent them from recurring in the future.
- **Implement lessons learned.** Share any advances made in how to do things better, even if they seem small (discovering shortcuts in apps, for example, or demonstrating a faster way to fill out paperwork).
- **Look ahead.** Ask what challenges and opportunities are coming down the road, and how the team can prepare for them. Here you might discuss new listings that are coming online or a busy day of brokers' open houses.
- **CEO update.** Talk about what you're reading, hearing, and seeing industry wide. This will help make team members industry experts for their clients, as they pass along insights.
- **Team status report.** Who's taking time off? Who's covering for them? Build awareness of what's going on within the team. In addition to making sure nothing slips through the cracks, this is an opportunity for people to get to know one another and build morale.

Now here's what not to do—and it's just as important:

- **Don't** let the meeting become a gripe fest. Venting is for the water cooler; this meeting is about making positive changes.

- **Don't** be the only problem-solver in the room. Everyone needs to contribute ideas about how to do things better, so be sure you give them the space to do so.
- **Don't** focus on solving the specific instance of any given problem. Instead, work toward preventing the problem from ever happening again. And if it's simply not preventable, create a ready-to-go solution for the next time it crops up.
- **Don't** assume anything is too small to be worth discussing. A solution may save only five or ten minutes, but those minutes add up over many transactions.

If you get pushback from your agents about participating in this process, that's a sign they're not team players. It doesn't matter if they're employees or independent contractors. If they use your logo, they represent your brand and have to play by your rules.

Stay on Offense

In real estate, everything changes constantly. The market, interest rates, macroeconomic trends, the weather, the season, local schools—it's all evolving and impacting your business. Running a successful team requires that you continuously gather information and pivot when necessary.

Pivoting means always staying on offense, not defense—being proactive, not reactive. Having a weekly team meeting is a key part of this. When you have a weekly meeting, you never have to call a meeting in response to something; the time is already set aside, and the agenda is all about thinking ahead.

Another pillar of proactivity is a stable, organizational environment for the team. Consistent expectations are one aspect of this, and they come from the people processes you learned about in Chapter 7. Strong leadership is another, which comes from building time into your schedule to think ahead; that makes it much easier to be strategic and decisive. This stability helps the team pivot with you and thrive during crazy times.

The ability to pivot quickly is what has allowed Dana's team to stay ahead of the competition in tough times, like the COVID-19 pandemic and the 2022 market downturn.

As soon as COVID lockdowns began, Dana's team created protocols and set up systems that allowed them to continue doing business despite the restrictions on showing homes. While other agents panicked or simply hit the pause button, Dana's team quickly figured out how to show homes by appointment, contact free. They requested that sellers not live in their houses while they were on the market, which reassured buyers that they could tour homes without any health risk. This kept the business active even through the toughest months of the pandemic.

When the market took a significant downturn following interest rate hikes in 2022, Dana's team pivoted again. With fewer active deals to pursue, they spent more time reconnecting with their networks and past clients. They couldn't change the market conditions, but they could keep cultivating relationships and reinforcing their role as trusted advisors. That way, when the downturn ran its course and people started thinking about buying and selling again, Dana's team would be top of mind.

Sometimes, the best offense is a great defense. That means patching holes in the boat, cleaning things up, and tightening your processes proactively.

In particular, failure to use your CRM properly is a major source of leakage in your business. Every contact needs to be not only entered into the system properly but also nurtured consistently over time—whether that person is a lead, a past client, or just someone in your sphere of influence. If you're not building relationships through regular follow-up, you're letting business walk in the front door and straight out the back.

For example, one agent recently told Jonathan about a man who visited an open house and greeted her by name. Seeing that she was drawing a blank, the man reminded the agent that he was a former client; she'd helped him buy a million-dollar home several years before. Then he said that he had recently moved, upgrading to an *$8 million* house. It turned out he was a musician who had hit it big.

This agent had missed out on an $8 million deal simply by failing to keep in touch with a former client. He remembered her, but she didn't bother to remember him or reach out to him in the years after he bought his first house. Of course he went with a different agent. Had she used her CRM properly (as we discussed in Chapter 7), that commission could have been hers.

Overall, the key to continuous improvement is to *ask questions* and seek answers. How could we do this better? How could we improve that process? What roadblocks are preventing us from closing an additional deal each week? What is the single biggest headache for each role?

The questions will vary widely depending on your geographical market, macroeconomic conditions, and so on. But as long as the team is asking questions and genuinely pursuing the answers, you'll keep getting better.

This will allow you to improve your performance even in a down market. For example, during the most recent downturn, Dana's team's total business was down—but its market share was up relative to its top competitor, so Dana knew the team was outperforming. Any market slump is stressful, but there's no need to panic, and Dana was able to communicate this to the entire team.

If they could maintain market share and ride out the storm, they'd be in peak form, ready to thrive when the market rebounded.

This learning culture is the key to sustained success. The market changes ceaselessly, and teams need to be quick to pivot to new circumstances. Everyone has to be smarter during the next three months than they were in the last three. And that goes for every component of their job: the industry, the market, the tools, the skills, and the relationships that make high-performing teams thrive.

PART IV

POST-SEASON ASSESSMENT

When the busy season dies down, it's time to take stock and see how well your business and your team performed.

Chapter 11

MANAGING THE NUMBERS

At the end of last year, Steve got an email from one of his coaching clients who leads a team. Over the holidays, she finally had time to sit down and crunch her team's numbers for the year. It turned out she was barely making any money from the team at all—basically breaking even. That's one thing if your team is just starting out, but she had been at it for three years. All her effort and investment were *not* paying off.

Worse, she didn't even know it until the end of December. Throughout the whole year, she was operating in the blind. She thought she was doing the right things to develop her team, but she had no idea if they were working. If she had known they weren't, she could have corrected her course a long time ago. Instead, months and months were wasted with nothing to show for it. How could this happen?

Well, you can't know your business until you know your numbers, and you can't leverage what you don't know.

Real estate agents love to ignore this inconvenient truth. For most of them, if they didn't have to file taxes, they wouldn't do any accounting at all. They would just go by their bank account balance—and even that, they only think about when it's empty. Nine out of ten agents don't even know their year-to-date gross commission income, the most basic measure of how your business is doing.

This self-defeating behavior comes from a combination of financial illiteracy and wishful thinking. If you don't know what your numbers mean or how to use them, they're scary. That's fair, and this chapter will help address that problem. What's more dangerous is the notion that if you pretend the numbers don't exist, they can't hurt you. That's just not true. They can, and they will. They probably already do.

Even when you're a solo agent, ignoring your numbers is a terrible idea. It's a major reason why so many agents struggle to achieve their goals. Even the successful ones are blind to the wasted effort, money, and opportunities in their business. But at least when you're on your own, you're only hurting yourself.

When you're leading a team, the risks are much greater. Other people's livelihoods are in your hands. You have a fiscal responsibility to pay your team and vendors on time. You're in charge of keeping the ship on course, and you can't do that if you don't watch your numbers regularly. It's not just a good idea—it's your obligation.

This chapter will get you started by making you aware of the questions you should be asking. We won't get into the details of how to find the answers—we could write a whole book on that. In reality, a lot of it comes down to finding the right financial professionals to help you and following their guidance. But to do that, you need to understand the big picture of what it means to know your numbers.

Set Up Data Collection Systems

Before we get into the financial weeds, it's worth reminding yourself why you started a team in the first place. Was it merely to cover your business expenses? Was it to improve your quality of life? Was it to make more income?

These are all very different outcomes, so judging your progress toward achieving them requires different metrics.

Ah, metrics. The very word scares off many agents. But you can't tell whether you're successful unless you measure the things you want to achieve.

For example, let's say you started a team to improve your quality of life—you were chained to your phone, missing family events, running yourself ragged, and you wanted that to stop. Now your team is up and running, and your income is good. But if you're working as many hours as you used to (or even more, with the added responsibilities) to make that income, you're not succeeding.

Collecting data is about tracking *everything* that matters, not just money.

That said, the first step in this process is to hire a good bookkeeper. There is no room for pushback here; for a high-performing real estate team, a top bookkeeper is *not optional.* If you're not serious about hiring one, there's no point in reading the rest of this chapter.

How do you find and hire a great bookkeeper? Start by asking around within your brokerage or other teams; it's best to use someone with experience in real estate accounting. They should be able to not just do the math but also understand your business, spot potential problems, and identify possible opportunities for improvement. Don't limit your search to your local area. You may want to stay within your state, as state laws can vary widely, and you want a bookkeeper who's familiar with yours. But like so many business relationships these days, this one will largely be handled via email and digital meetings.

Once you've landed this person, who will be worth their weight in gold (trust us), *listen to them*. Follow their advice about how to collect and send them financial data. They will track money coming in and its source, as well as money going out and where it goes. They'll also generate reports, particularly profit-and-loss statements and cash flow statements.

Most importantly, they should explain what these reports mean and ask questions about anything that seems odd. For example, they might point out that you're spending an unusually high amount on a certain item, which could mean there's potential for cost savings there. Or they might note that your revenues are up but your profit margin is down, which could indicate issues with efficiency.

In addition to tracking financial information with your bookkeeper, you'll also need to track some nonfinancial data, such as team member performance, market conditions, market share, and competition. Tracking such metrics will help you modify your planning to be more effective in the short and long run.

The key to success is to make this process as automatic as possible. Build it into your daily, weekly, or monthly routine. If you don't plan to perform this data collection yourself, make it a part of a team member's job and hold them accountable for delivering quality work on time.

All this goes back to our discussion in Chapter 7 about the importance of creating systems and processes; data collection is one of the business processes you need to build.

Understand What It All Means

All the data in the world won't do you any good if you don't understand what it means. As the business consultants say, data should become information, and information should lead to insights and then actions.

You'll want to block out time each month to review all your reports—both the finance-related ones created by your bookkeeper and the nonfinancial reports you're generating in-house. And when we say "block out," we mean it. As with all systems and processes, steadiness and predictability are your best weapons. Set aside the same time and same day every month to do a deep dive on these reports. Let nothing get in the way; treat this time as you would the most important client appointment.

Here are key questions to ask as you pore over the reports:

How are you doing relative to your goals?

- How does your income as a team leader compare to what you were making on your own?
- How much extra profit does the team generate for you after payroll and expenses are accounted for?
- Is the team achieving its overall production targets? How about individual members?
- Is your spending in line with what you expected in each major category? (Pro tip: Pay special attention to marketing and payroll, which will surely be your top two expenses.)

How are things changing from month to month, quarter to quarter, and year to year?

- Is revenue going up or down?
- What about expenses?
- Is the ratio changing?

Are you working in your strategic sweet spot?

- Closely track production, both in volume and number of transactions.

- Know where your business is coming from. How much is driven by repeats? By referrals? By marketing?
- Observe whether your transactions fall within the price-point parameters you set up. If they're not, it may be a sign that you or your agents are falling into old habits and chasing deals. The same goes for geographic guidelines.
- Make sure your fee is consistent for all clients. Don't allow discounts to become a crutch your team uses to win business; it will only come back to bite you if they refer you business or work with you again in the future.
- You should always know the total size of your market, your own market share, and that of your competition.

Pull Your Financial Levers

Once you know where your business stands, you can make decisions about where it should go. There are only so many things you can do to improve your team's financial health. It all comes down to increasing revenue and reducing costs.

The Revenue Side

The single most important thing you can do to increase revenue is *charge a full fee.*

You may want to read that sentence again, because we're passionate about it. Discounting will kill your business. Every time you agree to a discount, you're giving away your profit and compromising your retirement. You *must* charge a full fee if you want your business to thrive.

Charging a full fee helps define and legitimize your team. It forces team members to become the trusted advisors your clients want and need, and it prevents you from falling back into the deal-chasing trap. Let other agents bow and scrape for the next deal by settling for less. Your approach is that you are worth every nickel of a full fee, and you will prove it by providing superior value.

(If you think you can't do this, maybe we can persuade you otherwise. Steve has written an entire book on the subject, in collaboration with Chris Voss: *The Full Fee Agent.*)

Now, you're probably thinking that you can also grow revenue by increasing your transaction volume. Mathematically, that's true. In reality, it's an illusion.

Why? Because you can't directly control your volume. You control your fee—you can wake up tomorrow and say, "I charge 6 percent." You can't wake up tomorrow and say, "I sell 30 percent more houses."

You already learned this in Chapter 9: you and your agents don't decide when someone is ready to buy or sell. You don't decide whether the market is hot or cold. You don't set interest rates.

Transaction volume is a function of many factors, only one of which you control: the relationships you cultivate over time. Real estate is a long-term game. There's nothing you can do today that will bring in business tomorrow—no leads you can buy, no ad you can run that will make an immediate difference.

So if you want to increase your volume, the only thing you can do is . . . everything you've already learned in this book. Build the right culture, structure, and strategy for your team. Create robust systems, hire the right people, and market strategically. Always be searching for leaks in your boat, and plug them promptly. That way, the clients you do get will generate repeat and referral business—happily paying your full fee all the while.

The Cost Side

Now, let's talk about expenses.

Some are fixed, like your office lease. There's a contract with serious consequences if you don't pay up. In the short term, there's nothing you can do about fixed costs. Sure, there could be opportunities to trim them in the future, so you'll want to keep an eye on them—but this is not an easy lever to pull.

Here are some much more effective levers.

Commission Splits

Make sure you understand your splits with both your brokerage and your agents. Starting with the former, the truth is you probably don't have a lot of leverage; in most cases, the brokerage split is what it is. So the trick is to know what value you're getting from that split and exploit it for all it's worth.

For example, if you and some or all of your team works out of the brokerage even part of the time, your split is renting you an office. And not merely an office, but the many ancillaries that go with it: copying and printing, a kitchenette and coffee maker, office supplies, access to potential recruits, and so on. Chances are you're also receiving opportunities for continuing education and discounted rates for marketing and other materials.

These expenses add up. While you may not have much room to negotiate your brokerage split, it probably offers solid value in return. One of the numbers you should be tracking religiously is the dollar amount that goes to your brokerage. Compare this figure to the cost of the benefits we've just described. That way, you'll know what your split is buying you.

The split with your agents is usually more flexible, and this is an area in which most team leaders need to improve. We see splits that are all over the map. Often, team leaders offer overly generous splits to old friends or agents they perceive as stars. Or splits start out at a reasonable level, but every time an agent asks for an increase, the team leader gives in because they're afraid of losing the agent.

We're not saying all team members must receive exactly the same split, but remember: you're aiming to create a business that doesn't depend on any single team member. You're relying on process, not personalities. Develop a compensation plan that is financially sound, fair, and consistent. Start with your financial model—how much income do you need in order to be successful? Knowing this all-important figure, work backward using other variables (volume, transactions, number of agents, expenses) to create consistent compensation.

Salaries and Wages

The salaries and wages you pay non-agent team members are flexible. Yes, you have contracts to honor. But you also have the discretion to fire people, hire others, and change both hours and compensation plans.

For example, Dana recently decided to convert one full-time employee into an independent contractor without a guaranteed schedule. That way, compensation for the work would be variable instead of fixed. This eases financial pressure on the team in slow markets, when Dana could see that there wasn't enough work to justify a full-time job.

Clearly, such decisions shouldn't be made lightly. They deeply affect not only individual workers and their families, but overall team morale. On the other hand, if the team fails to perform at a sufficient level, everybody's job will go away. If you communicate the situation appropriately, as we'll discuss later in this chapter, your team will understand even when difficult changes are necessary.

Marketing

Marketing related to listings (photography and videography, brochures, Zillow ads, etc.) is a variable expense that rises and falls with the amount of business you do. You should track it on a per-listing basis to decide whether you're content with how much you're spending. Often, there are ways to trim this expense without compromising quality.

Then there's brand marketing, which we discussed extensively in Chapter 9. Brand marketing is one of the easiest expenses to adjust because you don't *have* to do any of it. Many agents and teams spend far too much on useless, nonstrategic marketing driven by ego or a copycat mentality. Obviously, we are all for cutting this sort of wasteful spending.

However, there's a huge caveat here. When it's done well, marketing does several important jobs for your team. It keeps you at the top of people's minds. It differentiates your team from solo agents. It reinforces your status as a group of knowledgeable professionals. Cutting too deep could have consequences for your brand recognition and reputation.

Adjusting your spending is a crucial lever for controlling the financial performance of your business. That said, use it carefully. There are always risks associated with these choices. It's up to you to make a judgment call based on the current market and economy, your forecast of the near future, and your risk tolerance.

Keep Your Team in the Know

Your team members don't need to be deeply involved in tracking business metrics and making financial decisions. Generally speaking, they're not qualified to do so, and it's not their responsibility. Most of them don't *want* to know the gory details. They just want to do their jobs, get paid on time, and feel appreciated.

That said, they do need to know some things—enough to understand the consequences of their actions, and the consequences of changes in the market. When teams are kept entirely in the dark, it creates the illusion that business performance has no bearing on their day-to-day efforts and vice versa. If they don't ever see the hard choices you're making or understand what drives them, they will resist when you try to make painful but necessary changes.

For example, one team leader we work with took a lot of grief from her team when she had to lay off two people. The market was down, and costs had to be cut somewhere or the business would fail—but her team didn't understand that. So she illustrated the trade-off for them: instead of laying off two people, she could cut everyone's pay by 15 percent. Did they want that instead?

Of course not. Once they understood the reality the business was facing and the reasoning behind the decision, the complaints ceased.

You don't need to share all the metrics—that's more than most people want to know, and it risks giving the impression that the team has more power over business decisions than they actually do. That said, here's what you *should* share:

- Total volume, in both dollars and transactions
- Percent of listings versus buyers
- Average sales price
- Average net commission (buy and sell side)
- Budgets
- Trends over time within the business
- Market share and competition
- Overall market trends

You may also want to share volume per agent, i.e., how much business each person is bringing in. This can be sensitive, and whether it's the right choice depends on the culture you want to create. On one hand, sharing this information encourages individual accountability. On the other, it can overinflate the egos of top-selling agents and lead them to demand more and collaborate less. It's up to you and what works best for your team.

You might also want to involve the team in solving certain problems that affect them deeply. For example, Dana consulted with her team when she had to trim their budget. Instead of deciding what to cut by herself, she asked what they would prefer to lose. From those conversations, she learned a lot about who and what was valuable to the team, which not only made the budget cut easier to implement but also gave her helpful information for future budgeting decisions.

Even though you're not providing full transparency, make financial decisions as if you were. In other words, ask yourself what would happen if people found out the things you're not disclosing—things like commission splits, salaries, or expenses. Would your decisions seem unfair, or would they make sense? Would you be able to justify them in a clear, logical way? If not, that's a warning sign that you need to rethink your choices.

Think about all the business considerations we've discussed so far, and your responsibility as team leader to track them. There's no way a rainmaker team leader can do all this *and* sell homes at the same time.

Every time you pull a financial lever, even a simple one, it creates a waterfall of work for your team. For example, anticipating a recent market and economic downturn, Dana's team decided to cut agents' assistants. It was the right move, but in order to keep carefully developed systems current and useful, the team had to change job descriptions, modify contracts, tweak job review procedures, and on and on.

That's why it's crucial to consider who will be responsible for all this work. As team leader, you're the ultimate strategic decision maker, but numbers and data may not be your greatest strength, and you have so much else to do. So consider delegating data collection and the implementation of financial decisions to someone else—a CFO or COO who *is* a numbers person.

Chapter 12

IMPROVING THE TEAM

It's very rare that the same team wins the Super Bowl two years in a row. (For trivia buffs, the feat was last accomplished by the New England Patriots in 2003 and 2004.) If you watch the sport, it's easy to see why.

Conditions change. Rosters change. Coaching staff change. The competition evolves, as do individual players—sometimes for the better, sometimes for the worse.

Well, the same is true for your business. You may think you have the dream team, and maybe you do right now . . . but nothing stays the same forever. Developing your team isn't a trek to a glorious summit, where you get to the top and you're done. It's a never-ending process of correcting, refining, and improving.

After all, the world around you is always changing. Your market never stands still, and neither do macroeconomic conditions outside your control. Your team members change too. They grow, their desires and priorities change, and sometimes they leave.

For all these reasons, it's crucial to periodically step back and assess your team. When you're in the thick of your busy season, small adjustments are all you can manage, as you learned in Chapter 10. But once or twice a year, when business is less intense, take the time to consider whether bigger changes are needed. In this chapter, you'll learn what questions to ask.

Limit Your Roles

Start your evaluation right at the top, with a look in the mirror. Consider the roles you're playing on the team.

Every team needs the following:

- **An owner** who considers the big picture—what kind of business to build and why
- **A leader**, whose job is to chart the course and steer the business
- **A rainmaker** who drives revenue generation and productivity
- **A manager** who focuses on efficiency, costs, execution, and details
- **Players,** whose task is to execute the business plan
- **Support staff** who make the players more effective

Look over that list again and think back to your days as a solo agent. You performed all these tasks, right? But all those responsibilities either limited your growth opportunities or took away your ability to lead a full, rich life. Or both.

That's why you formed a team—and if you want to reach the goals you made, you can't do everything.

The more you try to do, the worse your business and your life will be. You'll be pulled in too many directions and spread too thin to do any one thing well, and your reward will be burnout.

Plus, these different roles have different priorities; when one person plays all of them, it creates conflicts of interest. So as you grow your team, you must take steps to exit most of these roles and focus on what you do best.

It's pretty straightforward, really: at most, you should fill two of the roles listed above. And if you're reading this book, the owner role is not optional. That leaves you only one other role to fill, and in the vast majority of cases this comes down to leader or rainmaker.

If you're a salesperson at heart and don't have interest or the skills to become a strategic leader, aim to be an owner–rainmaker, and hire someone who can think strategically about the business for you. Conversely, if you want to be the strategic leader of your team and are willing to not top the sales chart, aim to be an owner–leader, and transition the responsibility for bringing in leads to your agents.

Now, step back and look at the past year. Which roles were you playing?

Probably way too many. Most team leaders try to be the owner, leader, rainmaker, *and* manager—and sometimes the support staff to boot. If that's you, ask yourself why.

Maybe you don't have the people you need—either not *enough* team members or not the *right* team members. If that's the case, make a plan to address the situation soon, before your next busy season. Add a new team member, train the people you already have to do what you need, or replace them with people who can.

Alternatively, maybe you're wearing too many hats because you simply haven't *let go* of the responsibilities that should belong to others now. This is extremely common. Agents like you who chose to build teams are smart, active, driven people who tend to get frustrated when someone can't perform a task as quickly or as well as they can.

But in order to grow, you have to let go. Doing everything is for solo agents, not business owners. Choosing not to delegate is choosing to remain stuck. It's choosing to work harder, earn less, and undergo more stress.

Is that the choice you want to make? Of course not.

So figure out what's preventing you from delegating. Make a plan to transfer the responsibilities you're hoarding to the team members who should have them, according to your business plan. Do whatever it takes to make it happen: update job descriptions, talk to your team, prepare them for change, and create mechanisms to hold yourself and them accountable.

One of the most common roles to get stuck in is that of manager. True, *somebody* needs to manage. But you can't do that *and* be the rainmaker or the leader, much less all three. When you're in the weeds of day-to-day operational details, it's impossible to also be focused on the big picture. On the flip side, if you're focused on the big picture, you don't have time for the details.

The temptation to backslide into managing is strongest during tough times. Even if you've been successfully delegating, when the market gets rough, you'll want to take control of everything again. You'll see your team struggling to sell and want to jump in and do it for them, because you know you can do it better. You'll see them struggling to implement strategic changes and want to get in the weeds of management.

That is a short-term solution, and it's shortsighted. You're a team now—everything is no longer on your shoulders. You don't need to do anyone's job for them, even if you can do it better. What you need to do is support them to do their jobs better.

Backsliding happens out of fear, and fear is a feeling, not a business model. When you start managing to feelings instead of the model, that's when things blow up.

Evaluate Each Individual

Having answered some challenging questions about your own role, it's now time to evaluate each team member. Here are the questions you need to be asking yourself:

- Do you have the right people on the team?
- Are they in the right positions?
- Are they being compensated sufficiently and in the right way?
- How can you help them grow?

During this process, you'll need to study every aspect of the business: buyer agents, listing agents, operations, and support services such as staging and photography.

Start with individual performance evaluations, which we discussed in Chapter 8. As we mentioned there, the key is to set clear expectations for each role as well as a structured, consistent evaluation protocol. Assess each team member against the following criteria:

Culture. Remember the values and principles you developed in Chapter 4? Every person on your team is either contributing to that culture or undermining it. In Chapter 4, we emphasized the importance of translating abstract values into observable behaviors, and this is why: so you can evaluate whether your team is fulfilling those expectations.

Productivity. Look at each person's performance against the metrics of their role. For agents, that's how many leads they converted, how many deals they closed, and how much income they produced. For other roles, the metrics may be different, but they're still important. Compare these figures to past performance and peer performance to get a sense of who is excelling and who needs to improve.

Client feedback. Are agents getting reviews? Are they positive or negative? Are there common themes that point to strengths and weaknesses of each team member? This is crucial information. You're trying to build a repeat and referral business, so the goal is to give every client an outstanding experience. Client feedback tells you who is succeeding at this and who is not.

Growth opportunities. As you evaluate each person, ask yourself if they're ready to take on more responsibility. As agents gain skill and confidence, they can take greater ownership over the client relationship. You should encourage this—it gives you greater freedom to focus on leadership and makes your team more valuable in the long run.

Outlook. Will each of your team members be able to perform at the same level in the coming year? Some may be expecting life changes that will affect how much they're willing or able to work, like an ailing parent or a kid going off to college. Be sure to ask so you can decide if you're adequately staffed.

Dana conducts the evaluation process in three steps. First, each team member performs a self- assessment using a structured form. The form isn't a surprise—it reflects the expectations that were set when they were hired, which are also in their job descriptions. Having each person assess themselves first makes the conversation easier; they're less likely to be defensive or surprised, because they already know what the issues are.

The second step is to respond to each evaluation in writing. This gives the other person the chance to digest your feedback in private first, where they can work through any emotions that might come up. It also creates a written record that could be important in the future if, for example, you have to let someone go and need to show that the decision was justified.

The third step is to have a frank conversation in person. Doing the written assessment and feedback first helps take the emotions out of what can be a stressful situation, so you can focus on solving issues and making improvements.

When it comes to helping underperforming team members, the key question to ask is how you can support them better. Do they need more training? Do they need to off-load some tasks to an assistant? Do they need better tools? There are some things you can provide, but in the end, each person needs to take ownership of their own performance and development.

For example, after a particular round of performance reviews, Dana decided to have her entire team join the weekly coaching call with Steve. This move offered everyone a chance to see more of the big-picture view of the market and industry. The change promoted increased discussion among team members and allowed Dana to give them more responsibility for their individual growth and productivity.

Manage for Business, Not Feelings

Most team leaders make poor personnel decisions—or fail to make decisions—because they're afraid of how people will feel about them. Is so-and-so going to be angry? Will they be happy? Might they leave?

Here's the problem: feelings are expensive. They have nothing to do with what's right for your business. If you're managing according to feelings, you're digging yourself into a hole.

Instead, as we mentioned earlier in this chapter, you need to manage according to your business model. That means you know how much revenue you must bring in and what your expenses are—and you do what's needed to increase the former and trim the latter until you're meeting your goals. Sometimes that's painful, but you can mitigate most wounded feelings through appropriate transparency.

Let's look at Dana's staging company as an example. These stagers have been with Dana for a long time. They're excellent at what they do, so they're the right people. However, when Dana recently studied their numbers, she saw that they weren't being deployed in the most efficient way.

The stagers had long worked on different pay scales determined by experience, with the most senior stagers earning more than twice the wage of junior stagers. Money was being wasted because senior stagers were often assigned to small homes or low-skill tasks, such as un-staging homes. Meanwhile, junior stagers were working on the most valuable homes—the ones with higher margins, where customer satisfaction was at a premium.

Dana ran the numbers and found that with smarter use of personnel, the team could save up to $1,500 per home. Multiply that by the number of transactions each year, and the money added up. It was clear that staff assignments had to change.

Dana knew some people might not be thrilled about this, but it was her job as leader to stick to the business model. Profit margins and high-quality service had to take priority over employees' feelings. To soften the blow, she explained the reasoning behind the change to her team and listened to their feedback, making sure they felt heard and respected. That was all it took to get the team on board with the new way of doing things.

Here's another example. Jonathan was recently charged with improving a large team that was actually underperforming its potential. Jonathan instituted a new business model—a road map for change and success—but it was clear that the existing agents were too set in their ways to change.

So he hired a new cohort of agents under a new set of expectations around behavior and production. None of it was optional; this was the way things would be going forward. He was creating a culture of accountability where there had been none.

Were there hard feelings about this change? Of course. Many of the old agents weren't happy about this new cohort and didn't mind saying so—but they could either get on board or leave. Their feelings were not allowed to dictate the success or failure of the business.

—

Even on a successful, established team like Dana's, change is sometimes necessary. During the recent market slowdown, the team—especially Dana as its leader—needed to be more proactive than they had been for years. Dana found that some team members were slow to change because they didn't fully understand the bigger picture of the business and the consequences of their daily behavior.

Dana realized she had two choices. She could revert back to the rainmaker role . . . but that would have been backsliding, retreating to her comfort zone. Instead, she assigned the team the responsibility of figuring out how to make changes that would get revenue and expenses back in line. Crucially, she also provided them the training, support, and other resources to make this happen.

At such times, it's helpful to return to the team's core principles. With roles clearly defined and assigned, team members know what they need to do. It's clearly laid out in their contract, after all. It's all about setting expectations and holding each other accountable.

Conclusion

Not long ago, a woman from Tennessee called Steve to see about working with him as a coach. She had a team of ten doing $65 million a year in sales—and she alone was bringing in $50 million of that. Shocked at the absurdity of those numbers, Steve asked how this had happened.

"Well," she explained, "at first it was just my husband and me, but then a friend of ours said she wanted to get into real estate, and then another . . . I guess it just happened organically." There was no plan, no structure, and no expectations—which led to a huge mess. A team of ten should do *at least* five times what a team of two can do, but hers was giving her only a 30 percent boost, and probably 0 percent of that was profit going into her pocket.

In real estate, when people think about building a team, they have the fantasy version in mind: a bunch of people who do what you want and make you money, without your having to manage or pay them. The reality usually looks a lot like what this Tennessee woman was dealing with: a bunch of people doing what *they* want and draining your time, energy, and bank account.

The purpose of this book is to save you from that fate. True teams—teams driven by strategy, structure, and collaboration—are powerful, so powerful that we believe they'll dominate the real estate landscape in the coming years. But building one is not for the faint of heart. It's not a short-term ploy to boost your income. It's a long-term investment in building a business that doesn't depend solely on you.

That's the only way you can scale your volume and still have a life. It's also the only way to build equity, so that your last deal isn't your last paycheck.

We've mentioned that endgame a lot, so let's talk about what it really looks like. For most agents, there's no succession plan. They work, and then they retire. Real estate is a job, not a business. Instead of building equity, they take out equity every year—and hopefully save some of that income for that retirement along the way. Even those that have a team rarely succeed in making the business outlast them.

It's not impossible to do—it's just that most agents have no idea how. There's shockingly little precedent for it in this industry. Because of that, real estate has to take its cues from other expert-based client-service industries, like the law and medicine.

Let's walk through the options for exiting your business, as well as what it takes to maximize its value. You'll see how everything you've learned in this book so far contributes to this endgame, where you have something of enduring value that someone else would actually want to buy.

What's Your Succession Plan?

There are four possible routes you can take to make your business live on—and continue paying you—even after you retire.

1. Pass it on to family.

If you have a child, niece, or nephew in the real estate business—or who wants to be in it—this can be a great option. The key is to bring them into the business early, long before you want to exit, so that they not only learn how to run it but also build support for their leadership among the team members. The more they actually contribute to the building of the business before you leave, the less likely the team will view their ascendancy to the leadership role as unfair or threatening.

You may simply give them the business, or there could be a financial aspect to the deal. If you choose to sell it, your successor probably won't have the capital to buy it from you outright. There are several ways to solve this. They could get a business loan to buy you out entirely, so you would receive a big payout immediately, and they would pay back the loan over time. Alternatively, you create an agreement where they buy shares from you little by little over time, and you continue receiving profits from the business according to your ownership share. Another possibility is to transfer whole ownership in exchange for a continued salary as an advisor.

2. Sell to your agents/employees.

Your employees—especially your agents—may be interested in taking over the business, especially if they've helped you build it from the start. As with the family succession plan, the key is to identify your successor(s) early and teach them to run the business well before you intend to leave. Your chances of success are greatest if you do this slowly over a year or more, so the team has time to get accustomed to the new leadership and work out the kinks while you're still around.

As far as financial arrangements, the options are essentially the same as with a family successor: an outright buyout funded by a loan, a slow buyout over time, or an annuity agreement.

3. Sell to an outside party.

This is still rare in real estate, but it happens all the time with private medical and dental practices. Another agent—maybe a competitor in your area, or a well-funded upstart—may want to take over your team entirely, perhaps even merge it with their own. In most cases, the buyer will want your team to stay, and you will probably need to offer the team a financial incentive to make sure they do. The purchase agreement may also include performance targets the business must meet for the transaction to be finalized.

The valuation of your business will depend on the timing of the transition and how much cash you receive up front. The more you get up front and the sooner you leave, the greater the buyer's risks are, so the lower the valuation will be. If you take less up front and stay longer to ensure a smooth transition, you'll command a higher total value.

4. Make referral agreements.

In this scenario, you're essentially just selling your database to another agent. They pick up your client relationships, and if a client does a deal with them, they pay you a referral fee; the more transactions you've done with that client in the past, the higher the fee. This is perhaps the easiest option and the most common one in real estate today, but it's also probably the least profitable because it doesn't capture the value of your business processes or personnel. That said, it's a quick exit and can be a double win if you do this with a younger colleague you want to see succeed.

The most important thing to remember is that if you're not preparing for one of these four options, you're on the road to the fifth alternative: close up shop and watch everything you've built disappear, with no pot of gold at the end of the rainbow. Even in that case, you still need to prepare by saving for retirement and investing those savings along the way. Otherwise, you'll be selling homes to pay the bills until the day you die.

The succession plan isn't just for you though. It's also for your team, who needs to know what will happen when you go away. They've put their heart and soul into the team and given up their individual identities as agents. Especially experienced agents who were involved in building the business may want to stay part of it even after you're gone. They need time to prepare for what's next, and you may need to provide an incentive for them to stay by sharing some of your payday.

Whatever your succession plan is, the transition will take time. You can't wake up one day and decide to retire and be gone tomorrow. You probably need at least three years to decide on your plan, execute it, and make sure the transition goes smoothly. And that's if you're already in a position to pass on leadership. If you're still a rainmaker, you'll need several more years to work your way out of sales and get your agents to stop depending on you for leads.

So start thinking about it now, even if you're just starting to build your team. Keep the endgame in mind as you grow so that when the time comes, you can make this transition as painless and profitable as possible.

Maximize Your Team's Value

In all four succession plan scenarios, you'll need to have a valuation done for your business to determine what it's worth. Dana has done this, and through the process, she learned a great deal about how to maximize her team's financial value. Here are the key things her valuation consultant looked at:

- **How involved you are in your business.** As you know by now, less is more. You're going to leave, so the less the business depends on you, the more valuable it is.

- **Where your business is coming from.** The higher the percentage of repeat and referral clients, the more valuable your business is.
- **Your financial performance.** They'll be looking for consistency in both profits and growth over time.
- **Your marketing performance.** Especially website traffic and SEO performance, which are good measurable indicators of your marketing strength.
- **Brand strength and reputation.** This includes reviews, references, and awards. The more positive feedback you can demonstrate from your clients and peers, the better.
- **Commission charged.** This is hugely important: Are you a full-fee team or a discount provider? The ability to successfully charge a higher fee indicates a strong underlying business that provides a high-quality client experience.
- **Contracts.** Are your contracts with your team members and vendors sound? Valuation consultants will look here for possible hidden risks that could undermine the business.
- **Processes.** These are what allow someone else to pick up the reins and carry on the business in the same way you did. The clearer and more robust they are, the more likely the business will continue to produce similar results, which makes it more valuable.

All these things flow from what you've been learning throughout this entire book. Processes? That's Chapter 7. Marketing? Chapter 9. Financial performance? Chapter 11. It's all here, and when you put together all the pieces, you create the ability to charge a full fee, maximize repeat and referral business, and extract yourself from the day-to-day operations.

That's how you grow your profits and get your life back at the same time—all while building a valuable asset that continues to generate value for you, even after you retire.

—

So what do you do now?

First of all, what you shouldn't do is worry about executing everything you've learned in this book right now. Rome wasn't built in a day, and your team won't be either. Remember, it's a cycle: pre-season planning, busy season execution, post-season assessment, and then back around to the start again.

Each cycle, you want to get a little better. Strengthen your leadership mindset. Refine your strategy. Establish a few more processes. Tighten up your finances. Shift a little more responsibility from yourself to your team. You can't do it all at once, especially in the beginning, when your team is still small.

Our advice is to use this book as a reference. At the beginning of each cycle, glance through it and choose a few things to focus on. Don't just set goals—it's too easy to let lofty ambitions get pushed into the back of a drawer and forgotten. Translate your focus into daily and weekly activities that you can put on the calendar, yours and your team's. Specific actions are the fuel that will move your team forward, one step at a time.

And if you need help holding yourself accountable or figuring out exactly what to do, reach out to us. Building real estate teams is what we do, and we'll be happy to help, whether it's through our group training programs or private coaching. Our goal—the whole reason we wrote this book—is to help real estate teams succeed.

If you're already a team member, we hope this book has empowered you to work more effectively with your teammates and leader. The more you understand about team structures, strategy, and dynamics, the more you can contribute to the team's success.

And if you still want to lead a team after all the warnings and hard truths we've delivered in these pages, you're one of the brave souls who can transform the real estate industry through the power of true teamwork. You have what it takes to build a lasting, thriving organization that empowers you—and your team members—to profit more *and* live better. That's a beautiful vision, and you can call on us to help you see it through.

About the Authors

Introducing Steve Shull . . .

Over the past thirty years, Steve Shull has been a guiding force in the realm of real estate coaching. He has devoted more than 60,000 hours to nurturing the growth of real estate professionals with one singular mission: to strategically position his clients for unparalleled success. The core of his coaching philosophy can be found in his bestselling real estate book, The Full Fee Agent (co-authored with Chris Voss).

Steve grew up outside Philadelphia and studied at the College of William and Mary in Williamsburg, Virginia, where he played football and graduated with a Bachelor of Science degree. His dream of playing in the NFL came true when he earned the rare opportunity to join the Miami Dolphins as a free agent. He played for four impactful years under legendary coach Don Shula, resulting in his designation as one of the tri-captains during the 1982 Super Bowl. When a knee injury ended his football career, Steve embarked on a new chapter, pursuing an MBA at the University of Miami. His subsequent tenure as an institutional fixed-income salesperson on Wall Street proved his adaptability and acumen. However, it was his migration to real estate that truly marked his destiny.

Steve's journey in this industry has encompassed an array of roles, from selling homes to co-founding a pioneering real estate enterprise. His counsel has been sought by major real estate brands, and his voice has resonated at prominent industry conferences, complementing his established coaching practice. Steve's unique perspective is the culmination of a multi-faceted immersion in nearly every aspect of the real estate realm.

In his upcoming book, Real Estate Is Not Rocket Science, Steve continues to distill his wealth of knowledge, offering invaluable insights to empower real estate professionals in their pursuit of excellence. Stay tuned as he once again reshapes the landscape of success in the ever-evolving world of real estate.

Dana Green

Dana Green has held the title of the top realtor in Lafayette, California, since 2008 and in the combined Lafayette, Moraga, and Orinda regions (Lamorinda) in California since 2010. Her unwavering passion and innovative approach to the real estate industry have positioned her as a trailblazer in Bay Area residential real estate. Dana was among the pioneers to adopt a "team" concept in the real estate business, creating a model where each team member plays a crucial and expert role in the transaction process. This strategic teamwork consistently yields meaningful real estate results by maintaining a dedicated focus on process, execution, and community engagement.

Boasting an impressive track record with over $2.5 billion in real estate sales and more than 1,100 homes sold, Dana Green has established herself as a market influencer, a natural connector, and a true master of her craft. She has received numerous accolades that reflect her exceptional contributions, including being honored as the MVP of Bay Area real estate by LuxeSF and RealTrends in 2019 and earning the title of Business Person of the Year by the Lafayette Chamber of Commerce in 2018. Dana's commitment to ethical business practices was recognized with the Better Business Bureau's prestigious Torch Award for Ethics in 2021. Additionally, she has been a recurring presence on the RISMedia Real Estate Newsmaker list and consistently ranks as one of the top mid-size teams on the RealTrends list of the Top 1,000 U.S. Agents. Notably, she has received the Five-Star Customer Service Award for an impressive eleven consecutive years.

Dana Green's impact extends beyond her professional success, as she has made significant contributions to the Lafayette community. Her deep-rooted relationships and commitment to creating positive outcomes benefit not only her business but also the wider community. Dana has generously donated over $500,000 to local non-profit organizations, underscoring her strong belief in giving back and maintaining a strong connection to the communities and industry she serves. She is currently serving her second term as a board member for Make-A-Wish Greater Bay Area, showcasing her dedication to making dreams come true. As an industry leader, Dana frequently serves as a guest speaker to realtors across the country and finds joy in teaching classes to her industry peers.

Dana Green's educational background includes a Bachelor of Arts in Communications with an emphasis in public relations from the University of the Pacific. Her commitment to excellence, ethical standards, and community enrichment continues to shape the real estate landscape in Lafayette and the broader Bay Area.

Jonathan Lack

Jonathan Lack is a serial entrepreneur and turnaround specialist focused on top-line growth for bottom-line results. He has over thirty years of experience in management and strategic planning in both consumer and business-to-business markets (e.g., startups, mid-size, and Fortune 500) in over fifteen industries.

Jonathan started consulting in residential real estate in 2018, initially helping the Carey Hagglund Condy team with its strategic planning, resulting in the firm becoming the #1 Compass Marin County team in 2022 and currently in 2023. Since July 2021, he has been the president and COO of the Beverly Hills-based Sally Forster Jones Group, one of the nation's top luxury residential real estate teams. Jonathan has conducted strategic planning webinars in conjunction with Steve Shull of Performance Coaching. He is currently working on a strategic planning book for real estate rainmakers titled You Can't Scale Chaos and is also the author of Plan to Turn Your Company Around in 90 Days.

Jonathan earned an MBA from the University of Pennsylvania's Wharton School of Business, an MA in International Relations from Johns Hopkins University's School for Advanced International Studies (SAIS), and a BA in Middle East Studies from the University of California at Berkeley.